Student Book

American Headway 4B

John and Liz Soars

OXFORD
UNIVERSITY PRESS

OXFORD
UNIVERSITY PRESS

198 Madison Avenue, New York, NY 10016 USA
Great Clarendon Street, Oxford OX2 6DP England

Oxford University Press is a department of the University of Oxford. It furthers the University's objective of excellence in research, scholarship, and education by publishing worldwide in

Oxford   New York

Auckland   Cape Town   Dar es Salaam   Hong Kong   Karachi
Kuala Lumpur   Madrid   Melbourne   Mexico City   Nairobi
New Delhi   Shanghai   Taipei   Toronto

With offices in

Argentina   Austria   Brazil   Chile   Czech Republic   France   Greece
Guatemala   Hungary   Italy   Japan   South Korea   Poland   Portugal
Singapore   Switzerland   Thailand   Turkey   Ukraine   Vietnam

OXFORD is a trademark of Oxford University Press.

Copyright © 2005 Oxford University Press

ISBN-13: 978 0 19 439276 1
ISBN-10: 0 19 439276 7

No unauthorized photocopying

All rights reserved. No part of this publication may be reproduced, stored in a retrieval system, or transmitted, in any form or by any means, electronic, mechanical, photocopying, recording, or otherwise, without the prior written permission of Oxford University Press.

This book is sold subject to the condition that it shall not, by way of trade or otherwise, be lent, resold, hired out, or otherwise circulated without the publisher's prior consent in any form of binding or cover than that in which it is published and without a similar condition including this condition being imposed on the subsequent purchaser.

Executive Publisher: Nancy Leonhardt
Editorial Manager: Jeff Krum
Editor: Mike Boyle
Art Editor (American Edition): Judi DeSouter
Production Manager: Shanta Persaud
Production Controller: Zai Jawat Ali

Printing (last digit): 10 9 8 7 6 5 4 3 2 1
Printed in Hong Kong.

ACKNOWLEDGEMENTS

The authors would like to thank Charles Lowe for his valuable contribution to the development of this project, and in particular for his ideas on the Music of English.

The authors and publisher are grateful to those who have given permission to reproduce the following extracts and adaptations of copyright material: p. 63 "Meet the Kippers" by Ray Connolly, *Daily Mail*, 18 November 2003. Reproduced by permission of Atlantic Syndication. pp. 70-71 "Fall asleep and you'll freeze to death" by Sarah Oliver, *Mail on Sunday*, 23 November 2003. Reproduced by permission of Atlantic Syndication. pp. 86-87 *The American West* 1840-1895 by Mike Mellor © Cambridge University Press, 1998. Reproduced by permission of Cambridge University Press. p. 88 "Jim and the Lion" from *Cautionary Verses* by Hilaire Belloc. Reprinted by permission of PFD on behalf of The Estate of Hilaire Belloc © The Estate of Hilaire Belloc, 1930. p. 102-103 "A Life in the Day of Mary Hobson" by Caroline Scott, *The Sunday Times Magazine*, 30 November 2003. Reproduced by permission of NI Syndication. p. 104 "That's Life" Words & Music by Dean Kay & Kelly Gordon © Copyright 1964 Bibo Music Publishers, USA. Universal Music Publishing Limited. All Rights Reserved. International Copyright Secured. p. 124 "A Darwin Award, Larry was a Truck Driver" from www.tech-sol.net as shown on 14 June 2004. Reproduced by permission of Mike Guenther, Techsol.

Sources: pp. 98-99 Based on copyright material "How's your timing" by Celia Brayfield.

Location art directors: Sally Smith and Mags Robertson
Art editing (International edition): Pictureresearch.co.uk
Cover concept: Rowie Christopher
Cover design: Rowie Christopher and Silver Editions

Illustrations by: Derek Brazell p. 68; Gill Button p. 89; Cartoon Stock pp. 64 (snake/Grizelda), (TV/Tony Hall), 77 (Timmy/Aaron Bacall), 97 (John Morris); Stefan Chabluk pp. 70, 82; Mark Duffin p. 124; Illustrations from "Jim" in Cautionary Tales for Children by Hilaire Belloc, illustrations copyright © 2002 by The Estate of Edward Gorey, reproduced by permisson of Harcourt Inc & Donadio & Olson Inc pp. 88 & 89;   Andy Hammond pp. 65, 80; Tim Maars pp. 96, 111.

Location and studio photography by: Gareth Boden pp. 63 (Martin), 73 (health club, B&B, vet's office, recycling center), 90, 91 (soccer); MM Studios pp. 115 (cell phone), 119 (Fair Trade produce)

We are grateful to the following for providing locations and props: Roger Noel & the children's football club, Forest Side Sports Ground p. 91; Oselli Ltd, Witney p. 90; Travelcare Travel Agents, Thame p. 90

We would also like to thank the following for permission to reproduce the following photographs: Alamy pp. 60 (Maria/J.Morgan), (Central Park/F.Skold), 90 (police officer/Bill Fritsch/Brand X Pictures); Alamy royalty free pp. 77 (teacher/SuperStock), 91 (student/D.Hammond/Design Pics Inc.), 123 (Iwish); Alaska stock: cover (highway); Capital Pictures pp. 78-79 all; Corbis pp. 61 (Indian wedding/J.Wishnetsky), 69 (Russia/S.Sherbell/SABA), 70 (M.Finn-Kelcey), 71 (Chukotka/N.Fobes), 76 (H. Armstrong Roberts), 82 (snow/Corbis Sygma), 86 (Seth Eastman, The Buffalo Hunter/ G.Clements), 125 (detail from The Creation of Adam by Michelangelo Buonarroti/World Films Enterprises), cover (CDs); Empics p. 71 (ChelseaFC/EPA); Geri Engberg p. 73 (self-storage sign); FPG: cover (surfer/Jason Childs), (blurry woman/Michael Goldman); Getty Images pp. 59 (forgive & forget/H. Grey), 61 (wedding line-up/B.Thomas), 62 (Vicki & father/K.Webster), 63 (Bill & Judy/T.Schmidt), 72 (crowd/M.Powell), 75 (Hulton Archive), 77 (30's teacher/W.Vanderson/Stringer/Hulton Archive), 84 (G.& M-D.de Lossy), 85 (painter/A.Roberts), 99 (R.Daly), 101 (couple/D.Pizzi), 101 (bench/Creaps), 101 (guitar/N.Daly), 121 (theatrers/A.Lyon), 122 (S.Justice); RC Hall p. 73 (AAA sign); Pal Hansen p. 103; Dennis Light p. 73 (auto body & cosmetic surgery); Masterfile p. 59 (male friends); Peter Newark p. 87; Photo Edit Inc. p. 81 (Michelle D. Bridwell); Punchstock pp. 58 (Comstock), 59 (excited women), 61 (drive-in wedding/Brand X Pictures), 61 (Pratima/Comstock), 63 (Sandra /Thinkstock), 92 (Photodisc Green), 94 (Photodisc Red), 121 (Soho), 121 (Piccadilly/Goodshoot); Redferns p. 104 (BBC); Rex Features pp. 66 (Silver Image), 67 (S.Cook), 72 (Oscar/D.Lewis); Karlene & Lowell Schwartz p. 73 (mortgage, hardware); Science Photo Library p. 101 (grandfather and child/Maximilian Stock Ltd); Liz Soars p 101 (sea tractor); South Tyrol Museum of Archaeology, Bolzano www.iceman.it pp. 82 (Iceman model), 83, 110; Still Pictures p. 69 (pyramids/H.Schwarzbach); Stockmarket: cover (globe/George B. Diebold), (cityscape/Lightscapes Inc.), (telephone body/Michael Keller), (asian face/Jeff Zaruba), (college students/John Henley); Superstock: cover (young people)

Contents

	Scope and Sequence	vi
7	Getting along	58
8	Going to extremes	66
9	Friends forever	74
10	Risking life and limb	82
11	In your dreams	90
12	It's never too late	98
	Getting Information	110
	Writing	120
	Tapescripts	134
	Grammar Reference	149

SCOPE AND SEQUENCE

Unit	Grammar	Vocabulary	Reading
7 Getting along p. 58	**Modals and related verbs 1** *able to, manage to, sure to, supposed to, allowed to* p. 58 **Spoken English** Declarative questions *Your father arranged your marriage?* Questions expressing surprise *You paid how much?* p. 61	Hot verb—*get* *We get along well. get angry, get to the truth, get out of doing the dishes* p. 64	"Meet the Kippers"—an article about grown-up children who won't leave home p. 62
8 Going to extremes p. 66	**Relative clauses** *that, who, what, whose, which* p. 66 **Participles** *the woman standing next to him a game played by four people* p. 67 **Spoken English** Adding a comment with *which* *I bought an umbrella, which was just as well.* p. 69	Adverb collocations Adverbs and adjectives *very cold, absolutely freezing, pretty nice* p. 72	"Chukotka, the coldest place on earth"—an article about a remote territory of Russia p. 70
9 Friends forever p. 74	**Expressing habit** *She's always borrowing my clothes. She'll spend hours staring into space. My dad would read me a story. He used to work hard, but now he's retired.* p. 74 *be used to doing* *He's a mover. He's used to working hard.* p. 74 **Spoken English** Intensifying compounds *scared stiff, dead wrong* p. 77	Homonyms *fine, match, book* Homophones *where* or *wear? knows* or *nose?* p. 80	"Friends past"—an article about the longest-running, most successful American sitcom *Friends* p. 78

Stop and Check 3   Teacher's Book p. 131

10 Risking life and limb p. 82	**Modal auxiliary verbs 2** *could have been might have done shouldn't have gone* p. 83 **Spoken English** Expressions with modal verbs *You might as well. I couldn't help it.* p. 85	Synonyms The story of Jim and the lion *buddies/friends delicious/tasty* p. 88	"Go West, Young Man!"—the story of settlers in nineteenth-century America p. 85
11 In your dreams p. 90	**Hypothesizing** *I wish I knew the answer. If only I'd told the truth!* p. 91 **Spoken English** Expressions with *if* *If all goes well … If worst comes to worst* p. 92	Word pairs *ups and downs pros and cons off and on slowly but surely* p. 93	"Have you ever wondered?"—the answers to some important questions in life p. 93
12 It's never too late p. 98	**Articles** *a/an, the, one,* zero article p. 99 **Determiners** *each, every, no, none, both, either* p. 99 **Spoken English** Demonstratives and determiners *What's that song? Every little bit helps.* p. 100	Hot words—*life* and *time* *get a life, kill time, right on time* p. 104	"You're never too old"—a life in the day of Mary Hobson, who earned her PhD at age 74 p. 102

Stop and Check 4   Teacher's Book p. 134

Listening	Speaking	Everyday English	Writing
Getting married—an Indian woman talks about her arranged marriage p. 61	The pros and cons of arranged marriages p. 61 Discussion—when should young people leave home? p. 62	Exaggeration and understatement *I'm totally crazy about you!* *I'm pretty fond of you.* p. 65	Arguing your case For and against *first of all …, not only … but also* p. 120
Extreme experiences—people describe their experiences in extreme weather conditions p. 69	Making descriptions longer p. 68 Talking about your experiences of extreme weather p. 69	The world around you—storefronts and signs *Hardware, Self-storage,* p.73	Describing places My favorite part of town *I'm a Londoner, and proud of it.* p. 121
A teacher I'll never forget—people describe a teacher who made a lasting impression on them p. 77	Discussion—a teacher I'll never forget p. 77 Discussion—your favorite TV programs p. 78	Making your point *The point I'm trying to make is …* *If you want my opinion …* p. 81	Writing for talking *What I want to talk about is …* p. 122
Hilaire Belloc's *Cautionary Tales for Children*—Jim, who ran away from his nurse and was eaten by a lion p. 88	It all went wrong! p. 85 Talking about children's stories p. 88	Metaphors and idioms—the body *bigheaded* *on its last legs* *a heart-to-heart talk* p. 89	Formal and informal letters and e-mails—Do's and don'ts *Hi Amber! How are things with you?* p. 123
The interpretation of dreams—Paul's amazing dream p. 96	Practicing a conversation p. 93 Describing your dreams p. 96	Moans and groans *I can't believe it!* *What a pain!* *It drives me crazy!* p. 97	Narrative writing 2 Linking words and expressions *As soon as, eventually, by this time, finally* p. 124
Happy days—people talk about what makes them happy and unhappy p. 101 A song—"That's Life" p. 104	Discussion—the different stages of life, and their pros and cons p. 101	Linking and commenting *Personally, anyway, hopefully* p. 105	Adding emphasis in writing People of influence *Michelangelo: sculptor, architect, painter, and poet* p. 125

7 Getting along

Modals and related verbs 1 • Hot verb *get* • Exaggeration and understatement

TEST YOUR GRAMMAR

1 Read the sentences 1–10 and underline the modal verbs. Rewrite them with a correct expression a–j.

1. You shouldn't wear red. It doesn't suit you.
2. May I make a suggestion?
3. You can smoke in the designated area only.
4. I can take you to the airport, after all.
5. You must obtain a visa to work in Australia.
6. You should always make an appointment.
7. You'll pass. Don't worry.
8. You can't walk on the grass.
9. I couldn't get through. The line was busy.
10. I won't discuss the matter any further.

   a. I'll be able to …
   b. I didn't manage to …
   c. You're sure to …
   d. You are required to …
   e. Is it OK if …?
   f. You're allowed to …
   g. If I were you …
   h. I refuse to …
   i. It's always a good idea to …
   j. You aren't permitted to …

2 **T 7.1** Listen and check.

3 Complete the lines a–j with your own ideas and compare with a partner.

I'll be able to come on Saturday, after all.

WE CAN WORK IT OUT
Modals and related verbs

1 **T 7.2** Read and listen to the two conversations. Who are the speakers? What are they talking about? Find all the examples of modal verbs.

1. A What the … where do you think you're going?
   B What do you mean?
   A Well, you can't turn right here.
   B Who says I can't?
   A That sign does. "Do Not Enter." Can't you read?
   B Hey, I couldn't see it, all right?
   A You should get your eyes tested. You're not fit to be on the roads.

2 **T 7.3** Listen to two similar conversations. What expressions are used instead of modal verbs?

3 Choose one of the conversations. Learn it by heart and act it out for the class with your partner.

GRAMMAR SPOT

1 Modal verbs have many meanings. Match a sentence in **A** with a meaning in **B**.

A	B
1. He can ski. 2. Can I go to the party? 3. You must stop at the intersection. 4. You must see the movie. 5. He must be rich. 6. I'll help you. 7. I won't help you. 8. You should exercise more. 9. It will be a good party. 10. It might rain.	ability advice obligation permission probability (un)willingness

2 Which meanings in **B** do these related verbs express?

> be able to   manage to   be allowed to   be sure to
> be supposed to   promise to   refuse to   have to
> be required to   be likely to   had better   Why don't you …?

3 What are the **question**, **negative**, and **third person singular** forms of these sentences?

> I can speak Japanese.   I'm able to speak three languages.
> I must go.   I have to go.   I've got to go.

Put the sentences into the past and future.

▶▶ Grammar Reference 7.1–7.3 pp. 149–151

2. **A** You won't tell anyone, will you?
   B Of course I won't.
   A You really can't tell a soul.
   B Trust me. I won't say a word.
   A But I know you. You'll tell someone.
   B Look. I really can keep a secret, you know. Oh, but can I tell David?
   A That's fine. He's invited too, of course. It's just that Ben and I want a really quiet affair, this being the second time around for both of us.

PRACTICE

Negotiating

1 Read the conversation. What is it about?

A *If I were you*, I'd swallow *my* pride and forgive and forget.
B Never! I *refuse to*.
A You'*ll have no choice* in the end. You *won't be able to* ignore each other forever.
B Maybe *I'll* forgive him, but *I'll never be able to* forget.
A *It has to be* possible to talk it over and work something out. You *have to* for the sake of the children.
B Oh, I just don't know what to do!

2 **T 7.4** Replace the words in *italics* with suitable modal verbs. Then listen and compare.

3 **T 7.5** Do the same with this conversation.

A I don't know if *I'll be able to* come tonight.
B But you *have to*. You *promised to*.
A Yeah, but *I'm not supposed to* go out on weeknights. My parents won't let me.
B *Why don't you* tell your parents that you're going over to the library to study?
A *Not possible*. Somebody'*s sure to* see me and tell them.
B We *have no choice but to* cancel the party then. Lots of kids *aren't able to* go out during final exams.

4 Practice the conversations with a partner.

Unit 7 • Getting along 59

Discussing grammar

5 Work with a partner. Which verbs or phrases can fill in the blank correctly? Cross out those which cannot.

1. I _____ be able to help you.
   a. won't   b. can't   c. might   d. may

2. Did you _____ keep it secret?
   a. could   b. manage to   c. able to   d. have to

3. You _____ be exhausted after such a long trip.
   a. must   b. can   c. had better   d. are sure to

4. The book is optional. Our teacher said that we _____ read it if we don't want to.
   a. can't   b. don't have to   c. don't need to   d. aren't supposed to

5. I absolutely _____ work late again tonight.
   a. will not   b. should not   c. might not   d. refuse to

6. _____ hold your breath for more than a minute?
   a. Are you able to   b. Can you   c. May you   d. Could you

7. _____ tell me where the station is?
   a. May you   b. Could you   c. Are you able to   d. Can you

8. _____ I have some more dessert?
   a. Could   b. May   c. Will   d. Would

9. Will you _____ go on the trip with us?
   a. can   b. be able to   c. be allowed to   d. may

10. You _____ go to England to learn English.
    a. should   b. don't have to   c. shouldn't   d. could

11. You _____ worry so much. Everything will be OK.
    a. couldn't   b. shouldn't   c. don't have to   d. can't

12. I _____ call home.
    a. 'd better   b. ought to   c. am likely to   d. had to

6 Rewrite the sentences using the words in parentheses.

1. I just know it'll rain this weekend. (*sure*)
2. He passed his driver's test after three tries. (*manage*), (*succeed*)
3. Can you tell which twin is which? (*able*)
4. My parents say I can't have a puppy. (*allow*), (*let*)
5. You should take it back and complain. (*If*), (*better*)
6. I should wear a suit for work, but I often don't. (*supposed*)
7. You can't tell anyone about it. (*better*), (*promise*)
8. He said he wouldn't turn down the volume. (*refuse*)

Exciting news

7 Read one side of a telephone conversation between Maria and Rebecca.

R Hello?
M …
R Maria, hi! Why all the excitement?
M …
R Yes, I can. I remember you doing it in the coffee shop. It was the one in the *Post*, wasn't it? Didn't you have to name a bunch of capital cities?
M …
R No way! I don't believe it. What's the prize?
M …
R You must be kidding! That's great. For how long?
M …
R Well, you should be able to do quite a lot in three days. And the Ritz Carlton! I'm impressed! Doesn't that overlook Central Park?
M …
R I thought so. Can't say I've been there, of course.
M …
R What do you mean? How would I ever be able to?
M …
R You can't be serious! You know I'd love to! But why me? Surely you should be taking David.
M …
R Oh, I'm sorry! I didn't know. When did this happen?
M …
R Well, what can I say? How could I possibly refuse an offer like that?
M …
R I definitely will!

Can you work out the answers to these questions?
- Why is Maria so excited?
- Where is she going?
- What is the relationship between Maria and David?

8 What do you think Maria's exact words were in the conversation? Practice it with a partner.

9 **T 7.6** Listen to the actual conversation between Maria and Rebecca. Compare your ideas.

LISTENING AND SPEAKING
Getting married

1 Look at the photos of three weddings and describe them.

2 What do you think are good reasons to get married? What do you think are bad reasons? Discuss ideas with the class.

3 This is Pratima Kejriwal, an Indian woman who had an arranged marriage. What would you like to know about her marriage? Write questions with a partner.

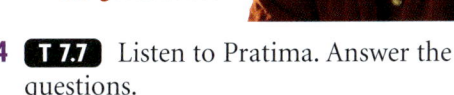

Who arranged the marriage?
How old was she when she got married?

4 **T 7.7** Listen to Pratima. Answer the questions.
 1. Which of the questions you wrote were answered? What are the answers?
 2. How did Pratima's father find the two men?
 3. What did he want to know about them?
 4. What were the similarities and differences between the two men?
 5. Why did her father choose Shyam and not the first man?
 6. Why did Shyam dress badly?
 7. What happened between the time of the interview and the wedding?
 8. How do you know that Pratima believes in arranged marriages?

SPOKEN ENGLISH Other question forms

1 What is unusual about these questions from the interview?

> And your father arranged your marriage?
> And this one your father chose?
> He had to?

These are *declarative questions*, and are used when the speaker thinks he/she has understood something, but wants to make sure or express surprise. Find more examples in the tapescript on page 134.

2 Look at this question from the interview.

> For my sister, my elder sister, he saw over one hundred men before …
> **He saw how many?**

What emotion does this question form express? Make similar questions in reply to these statements.
 1. My friends went to Alaska on vacation. **They went …?**
 2. I got home at 5:00 this morning.
 3. I paid $300 for a pair of jeans.
 4. I met the president while I was out shopping.
 5. He invited me to the White House for lunch.

T 7.8 Listen and check.

What do you think?

- Do you think arranged marriages are a good or bad thing? Work in groups and make a list of all the advantages and disadvantages that you can think of.
- What other ways do people meet marriage partners? Do you believe some ways are better than others? If so, which?

Discuss your ideas with the class.

 WRITING Arguing your case—For and against *p. 120*

READING AND SPEAKING
Meet the kippers

1. When do young people usually leave home in your country? Why do they leave? Work in two groups. List reasons for and against leaving home when you grow up.

   Group A Make a list from the children's point of view.
   Group B Make a list from the parents' point of view.

   Share ideas with the class.

2. Read the introduction to the article and answer the questions.
   1. Who are the kippers? What do they refuse to do?
   2. What do the letters stand for?
   3. What exactly does "eroding retirement savings" mean?
   4. What does "leave the nest" mean?

3. Read about two kipper children and answer the questions in your groups.
   Group A Read about **Vicki**.   **Group B** Read about **Martin**.

   1. Who does she/he live with? Do they get along together?
   2. Why does she/he still live at home?
   3. Has she/he ever lived away from home?
   4. What advantages and disadvantages are mentioned?
   5. What do her/his friends say?

   Work with someone from the other group and compare the two children. Who do you think is the most spoiled?

4. Read about two parents of kippers, Bill and Sandra. Compare their views.
   1. Who is happy with the arrangement? Why? Who is not? Why not?
   2. Who is at their "wits' end"?
   3. What do they say about foreign travel?
   4. What do they say about money?

Vocabulary work

Complete the sentences with words from the text. Who does each sentence refer to?

1. She isn't able to r_____ an apartment.
2. He couldn't a_____ to pay o_____ his d_____.
3. Her friends are always s_____ for c_____ because they have to pay h_____ rents.
4. She c_____ to the phone b_____.
5. She doesn't c_____ him r_____ because he wouldn't pay it.
6. He r_____ u_____ $8,000 in debt.
7. He sponges o_____ his mother in many ways.
8. He can s_____ all his s_____ on enjoying himself.
9. He believes that m_____ isn't e_____.

What do you think?

- Check your list of reasons from Exercise 1. Which were mentioned?
- What's your opinion of Vicki and Martin?
- Do you sympathize more with Bill's views or Sandra's? Why?
- Is it possible to "grow up" while still living at home?
- Do you know any kippers?

MEET

Who are they?
They're the children who just WON'T leave home.

Kippers is an acronym for "Kids In Parents' Pockets Eroding Retirement Savings." Or, to put it another way, it refers to all those grown-up children who stay at home into their 20s and 30s, unwilling or unable to leave the nest.

THE CHILDREN

VICKI SARGENT, 30, lives with her father, Norbert, 65.

IF I WASN'T living at home, I wouldn't be able to afford to live in such a beautiful house. I would only be able to rent a room in an apartment. This way I have my father for company and money for a social life. It's just too comfortable to move out.

My dad and I get along well. We usually have dinner together, and if I'm not out, I'll spend the evening with him watching TV. He spoils me a lot and treats me at least once a week to dinner at a nearby restaurant.

My friends don't get it. They say I'm living in a bubble away from the real world, and I guess they're right. But they also admit they're jealous—they are always so strapped for cash because of their high rents. I don't pay my father any rent but I buy the food and contribute to the phone bill.

Apart from three months when I went traveling in my early 20s, I have never lived away from home.

THE K.I.P.P.E.R.S

MARTIN GIBBS, 28, lives with his parents Kathy, 52, and Robert, 54.

I HAVE TO admit that I'm spoiled at home, so it's hard to imagine moving out. My mom always has my breakfast on the table when I get up in the morning. We all get along really well together, although my parents can get on my nerves when they tell me what to do. But I'm sure I get on their nerves too sometimes.

At 23, I moved out for two years. I lived with a friend for a short time, then went traveling in Asia. It was an amazing experience, but I got into debt, about $5,000, and I had to come back and live at home again so that I could afford to pay it off. My parents don't charge me rent, so I can spend all of my salary on enjoying myself. Sometimes girls call me a "mama's boy," but I think they like it. It's a nice, cozy place to bring girls back to because there is always an open fire and something cooking in the oven.

THE PARENTS

BILL KENNEDY tells why his children, Anna, Simon, and Andrew can stay as long as they like!

NO ONE TOLD ME, but it seems I was the father of kippers for years, without knowing it. My three children all lived at home well into their late 20s. I know there'll be some parents at their wits' end with their "lazy kids sponging off them." Actually, we don't want an empty nest. What puzzles me is why parents should ever want their children to leave home at 18. My wife Judy and I made it very easy for them to stay with us. It allowed them to postpone growing up. And it helped us postpone getting old. Honestly, I would happily forfeit any number of retirement perks—golfing, snorkeling, trips to Paris, Peru, or wherever—for just a few more years with our children at home. And why? Because money isn't everything. Family is.

SANDRA LANE, 49, says it's domestic hell with her son, Alan, 27.

THE FRIDGE IS the main issue. He's always helping himself to some tidbit that I've been saving for dinner. And he puts the empty milk cartons back! The phone is another cause for complaint—he's always getting calls from his buddies, but when I get angry he just says I should get a cell phone. And he borrows the car without asking, and so I suddenly find myself unable to go out. He's been living at home since he graduated from college five years ago. By the time he finished school he had racked up $8,000 in debt. I can't charge him rent. There's no point. He couldn't and wouldn't pay it. But he's always got money for clothes and nights out. I'm at my wits' end with it all. I had been planning to go on a dream cruise as soon as Alan left home. Now that's all it can be—a dream.

Unit 7 • Getting along 63

VOCABULARY AND SPEAKING
Hot verb *get*

1 The verb *get* is very common in English. It has many different uses. Here are some examples from the texts on pp. 62–63.

1. My dad and I **get along well**.
2. My friends don't **get it**.
3. ... my parents can **get on my nerves** ...
4. ... it helped us postpone **getting** old.
5. ... when I **get** angry ...
6. ... he's always **getting** calls from his buddies ...
7. ... he just says I should **get** a cell phone.
8. ... he's always **got** money for clothes ...

Replace the words in **bold** with one of the expressions from the box.

> annoy/irritate me   buy   become
> receiving   growing   understand
> have a good relationship   has

Talking about you

2 Ask and answer these questions with a partner.

1. Do you get along with your parents?
2. What have you got to do when you get home tonight?
3. How do you get to school?
4. What time do you usually get to school?
5. When did you last get angry? Why?
6. Name three things you've got in your bag.
7. If you have a problem with your computer, who do you get to help you?
8. How often do you get your hair cut?
9. In what ways is your English getting better?
10. What are two things that always get on your nerves?

Work together to rewrite the questions without using *get*. Is *get* generally more formal or informal?

Phrasal verbs with *get*

3 *Get* can combine with many particles to make phrasal verbs. Complete each group of sentences with the same particle from the box below. (Careful, only six of the particles are used.)

| to   away   into   off   on   out   over   around   through   up |

1. You always get How did our secret get I got a great book	_____	of doing the dishes. It's not fair. ? Everyone knows now! of the library. You can borrow it after me.
2. The police finally got Just to get All his teasing got	_____	the truth about the robbery. work I have to take three buses. me. It really hurt my feelings.
3. It took forever to get He still can't get I can't get	_____	the flu. the death of his pet dog. how much your children have grown!
4. He got We got I had to get	_____	to 300 pounds before he went on a diet. to page 56 in the last class. at 5 A.M. to catch the plane.
5. I couldn't get I tried to get Sue got	_____	to Joe. His phone was busy. to her, but she ignored my advice. the test quickly, but I took forever.
6. You can always get I'm sorry. I haven't gotten I can't see how we can get	_____	the rules if you hire a good lawyer. to replying to your invitation yet. this problem. It's a difficult one.

"How is the cat getting along with your new pet snake?"

"It's the only way I can get the kids to take notice of me."

EVERYDAY ENGLISH
Exaggeration and understatement

1 What is strange about these cartoons?

"I'm pretty fond of you."

"I worship the ground you walk on."

2 Which of these declarations of love are exaggerated? Which are understated?

I'm totally crazy about you.   We enjoy each other's company, don't we?
I kind of like you, you know.   I adore you and I can't live without you.

3 Match a line in **A** with a line in **B**. Use your dictionary to look up new words.

A	B
1. ☐ I'm dying for a cup of coffee.	a. Yes, it was a nice little break, but all good things must come to an end.
2. ☐ His parents are pretty well off, aren't they?	b. That's for sure. He's as dumb as dirt.
3. ☐ You must have hit the roof when she told you she'd crashed your car.	c. I wouldn't mind one myself.
4. ☐ I think Tony was a little rude last night.	d. No kidding! He was completely out of line!
5. ☐ I can't stand the sight of him!	e. I guess it is a little chilly.
6. ☐ He isn't very smart, is he?	f. Yeah, they do seem to get along well.
7. ☐ I'm fed up with this weather! It's freezing.	g. Yeah. I'm a little tired, too.
8. ☐ Well, that was a fantastic trip!	h. Well, yeah, I was a little upset.
9. ☐ I'm wiped out. I've got to go to bed.	i. You can say that again! They're totally loaded!
10. ☐ They're obviously madly in love.	j. I have to say I'm not too big on him, either.

4 **T 7.9** Listen and check your answers. Which words are examples of exaggeration? Which are understatements? Practice the conversations with a partner.

5 Work with a partner. Read aloud these understated remarks and give exaggerated replies.

> I'm pretty tired. Can we finish this tomorrow?
>
> Yeah, let's stop now. I'm completely exhausted.

1. Is that a new watch? I bet that cost something.
2. It's a little chilly in here, don't you think?
3. These shoes aren't bad, are they?
4. Can we pull over at the next rest stop? I could use something to eat.

T 7.11 Listen and compare.

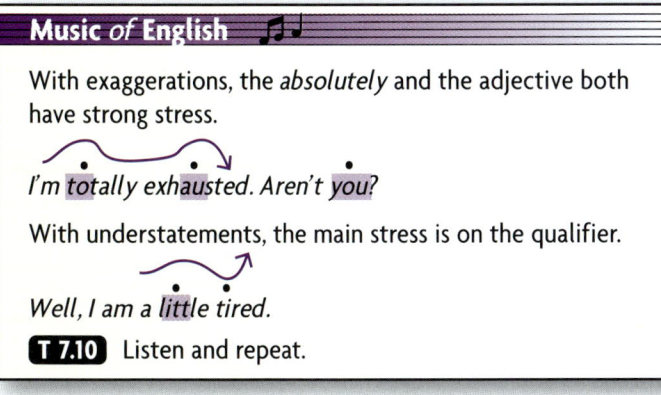

Music of English

With exaggerations, the *absolutely* and the adjective both have strong stress.

I'm totally exhausted. Aren't you?

With understatements, the main stress is on the qualifier.

Well, I am a little tired.

T 7.10 Listen and repeat.

8 Going to extremes

Relative clauses • Participles • Adverb collocations • The world around you

TEST YOUR GRAMMAR

1 Complete the sentences with one of the words below.

| who   which   where   what   when   whose |

1. The man _____ you met was my brother.
2. My other brother, _____ lives in London, is a teacher.
3. He suddenly quit his job, _____ came as a shock.
4. He says that _____ he wants to do is move to Australia.
5. His girlfriend, _____ parents live in Melbourne, is delighted.
6. They're not sure exactly _____ or _____ they're going.
7. Their house, _____ they bought last year, is up for sale.
8. The house _____ I want to buy is on Acacia Avenue.

2 In which sentences can the relative pronoun be replaced by *that*?

3 <u>Underline</u> the present and past participles in these sentences. Rewrite them with relative pronouns.

1. The woman standing next to him is his wife.
2. Most TVs sold in the US are imported models.

PILOT SUPERSTAR
Relative clauses and participles

1 What do you know about John Travolta? Look at the photos and read the text quickly. What do you learn about his lifestyle? What is his passion?

2 Read the text again and complete it with the clauses a–j.

   a. which is built
   b. who lives
   c. who isn't full of himself
   d. where the super-rich can commute
   e. including a Gulfstream executive jet
   f. whose $3.5 million mansion
   g. Walking out of his door
   h. which means
   i. previously owned by Frank Sinatra
   j. most of whom share

   T 8.1 Listen and check your answers.

JUMBOLAIR

HOME OF JET PILOT JOHN TRAVOLTA

3 Answer the questions.
1. What kind of people live in Jumbolair?
2. Does John Travolta own three planes or more than three?
3. Who owned the Boeing 707 before Travolta?
4. What is Travolta's home like?
5. Why is it called "the ultimate boys' fantasy house"?
6. What is "apt" about the name of his son?
7. Why don't the neighbors complain about the noise?
8. Does Travolta behave like a typical movie star?

Welcome to JUMBOLAIR, Florida—the world's only housing development (1)_____ to work by jet plane from their own front doors.

Jumbolair's most famous resident is Hollywood movie star John Travolta, (2)_____ is big enough to park a row of airplanes, (3)_____ , a two-seater jet fighter, and a four-engine Boeing 707, (4)_____.
Travolta holds a commercial pilot's license, (5)_____ he's qualified to fly passenger jets. He can land his planes and taxi them up to his front gates. His sumptuous Florida home, (6)_____ in the style of an airport terminal building, is the ultimate boys' fantasy house made real. As well as the parking lots for the jets, there is a heliport, swimming pool and gym, stables for 75 horses, and of course a 1.4-mile runway.
Family man Travolta, (7)_____ with wife Kelly, daughter Ella Bleu, and aptly named son Jett, flies daily from his home when filming. (8)_____ and into the cockpit, he is airborne in minutes. His neighbors, (9)_____ his love of aviation, don't seem to mind the roar of his jets. They say that it's nice to meet a superstar (10)_____. "He's just a regular guy, very friendly," says one neighbor.

GRAMMAR SPOT

Relative clauses
Relative clauses are like adjectives. They give more information about nouns.
*We have a German neighbor **who comes from Munich**.*

1 Read these sentences aloud, paying attention to the punctuation. Underline the relative clauses.
I met a man who's a pilot.
My friend Adam, who lives in London, is a pilot.
The house which you walked past is my aunt's.
My aunt's house, which I don't like, is very modern.

2 In each pair of sentences, which relative clause …
… tells us exactly *who* or *what* is being talked about?
(A **defining** relative clause)
… gives us an extra piece of information?
(A **nondefining** relative clause)
Explain the use of commas. How do they affect the pronunciation?

3 In which sentence in Exercise 1 can the relative pronoun be omitted? Why?

Present and past participles
Underline the participles in these sentences. Which are adjectives? Which are present and which are past?
Who is that boring man standing at the bar?
The curtains and carpets included in the sale were old and worn.
They own four houses, including a ruined castle in Scotland.
Having lost all his money, he was a broken man.

▶▶ Grammar Reference 8.1–8.2 pp. 151–152

PRACTICE

Pronunciation and punctuation

1 Work with a partner. Read the sentences aloud, then write in the correct punctuation where necessary.
1. The area of New York I like best is Soho.
2. My father who's a doctor plays the drums.
3. The book that I'm reading now is fascinating.
4. Paul passed his driver's test on the first try which surprised everybody.
5. People who smoke risk getting all sorts of illnesses.
6. I met a man whose main aim in life was to visit every capital city in the world.
7. The Channel Tunnel which opened in 1995 is a great way to get from England to France.
8. What I like best about work are the vacation days.
9. A short bald man seen running away from the scene of the crime is being sought by the police.

T 8.2 Listen and compare your pronunciation. Repeat the sentences.

Discussing grammar

2 Read these sentences and decide which need *more* information to make sense.

1. People _____ live longer.
2. The apple tree in our garden _____ needs to be cut down.
3. She married a man _____.
4. The Great Barrier Reef _____ is the largest coral reef in the world.
5. Did I show you the photos _____?
6. Let me introduce you to Kim Lee _____.
7. I'm looking for a book _____.
8. I was speaking to someone _____.

3 Add these sentences to the ones in Exercise 2, using relative clauses. Leave out the pronoun if possible.

People who do regular exercise live longer.

a. She works in our Paris office.
b. You know this person.
c. We took them in Barbados.
d. She met him on vacation in Turkey.
e. It teaches German grammar.
f. They do regular exercise.
g. My grandfather planted it 60 years ago.
h. It is situated off the coast of Australia.

Depress -ed or *depress -ing*?

4 Which words in **B** go with the topics in **A**?

A	B
1. test results	challenging/challenged
2. a vacation	shocking/shocked
3. gossip	disappointing/disappointed
4. a trip	boring/bored
5. a job	relaxing/relaxed
6. a hard luck story	exhausting/exhausted
7. a TV documentary	amusing/amused
8. a social situation	embarrassing/embarrassed

T 8.3 Listen to conversations about the topics. For each, say how the people feel and why. Use the adjectives in **B**.

"It's raining again!"
"Oh, no! Another miserable day when we're stuck indoors."

She's depressed.   *The weather is depressing.*

5 Complete each pair of sentences with the correct form of the same verb, once as a present participle (*-ing*) and once as a past participle.

1. I hurt my leg _____ football.
   Bridge is a card game _____ by four people.
2. It says _____ *in Korea* on my camera.
   I have a job in a cafe _____ sandwiches.
3. I've spent the whole morning _____ an essay.
   On the wall was some graffiti _____ in big letters.
4. Items _____ on sale cannot be returned.
   I've spent all my money _____ Christmas presents.
5. The police caught the burglar _____ into a house.
   Careful! There's a lot of _____ glass on the floor.

Making descriptions longer

6 Add *all* the words and phrases from the box to this short sentence to make one long sentence.

A woman was sitting in her garden.

| lost in her thoughts | lazily going from rose to rose | beautiful |
| country | watching a bee | gathering honey | young |

T 8.4 Listen and check.

7 Work with a partner. Choose two sentences and make them longer. Read them aloud to the class. Who has the longest sentence?

1. *A man walked along the road.*
2. *Peter has a farmhouse in the country.*
3. *Ann Croft, the actress, was seen having lunch in a restaurant.*
4. *The trip to Hawaii was a disaster.*
5. *A boy found a wallet on Main Street.*

T 8.5 Listen and compare your ideas.

LISTENING AND SPEAKING
Extreme experiences

1 What's the coldest, hottest, or wettest you've ever been? Where were you? What were you doing? Work in groups, and then tell the class.

2 You are going to listen to Simone and Anna recalling their extreme experiences of heat and cold. Look at the words and discuss what you think happened.

Simone	Anna
a night club	a tram
the pyramids	scarves
sunrise	frozen nostrils
a taxi	an anonymous landscape
a motorcycle	huge apartment blocks
heat exhaustion	an old lady
salt tablets	bonfires

3 **T 8.6** Listen to Simone and answer the questions.
1. Where was she?
2. What was the temperature?
3. What did she do that was stupid or silly?
4. What kind(s) of transportation did she use?
5. Where was she going to? Why?
6. What did she see when she arrived?
7. Who did she meet? Was this person helpful?
8. How did the temperature affect her?
9. What happened in the end?

4 Guess the answers to the same questions about Anna's story. Use the words in Exercise 2 to help.

5 **T 8.7** Listen and answer the questions in Exercise 3 about Anna. Compare your ideas.

Language work

6 Complete the sentences with the adverbs used by Simone and Anna.

| completely   dramatically   exactly   extremely |
| profusely   properly   really   seriously   stupidly |

1. It was _____ hot and _____ we decided to go dancing.
2. We were sweating _____.
3. The temperature rises _____.
4. My brain wasn't working _____.
5. It was _____ anonymous, this landscape.
6. They all looked _____ the same.
7. I was beginning to _____, _____ panic.

SPOKEN ENGLISH Adding a comment

In conversation we can add a comment with *which* as an afterthought. This often expresses our reaction to what we have said.
  He gave me a ride home, which was nice.

1 Add a suitable comment from **B** to Simone's and Anna's comments in **A**. Sometimes more than one is correct.

A	B
1. We went dancing in temperatures of over 40°C,	which is hard to believe.
2. My friends were worried I'd get lost,	which was just amazing.
3. We visited the pyramids at sunrise,	which was a pretty stupid thing to do.
4. My nostrils actually froze,	which was no joke.
5. This motorcycle broke down,	which was no laughing matter.
6. The old lady didn't understand a word I said,	which was understandable.
	which is hardly surprising since my Russian's lousy.

T 8.8 Listen and check. Practice saying the comments with a partner.

2 Write sentences ending with a comment from **B**. Tell the class.
  I missed the last bus home, which was no laughing matter.

READING AND SPEAKING
Chukotka, the coldest place on earth

1 Look at the photos. What do you think links Roman Abramovich with the two places?

2 Read these facts about Chukotka, the coldest place on earth. Which facts do you find surprising? Which are not surprising? Why? Discuss with a partner.

> The people don't use fridges or freezers.
> There's no crime.
> It is a remote territory of Russia.
> Its capital, Anadyr, is a boomtown.
> It's too cold to play soccer.
> One of the world's richest men lives there.
> The only flowers are the plastic ones.

3 Read the article quickly. Answer these questions and share information with the class.
   1. There are five headings. What does each refer to?
   2. For each fact in Exercise 2 find some related information.

> The people don't use fridges or freezers. They hang their meat outside in plastic bags.

4 Read the article again and answer the questions.
   1. Where exactly is Chukotka?
   2. What is the climate like? In what ways does it have "weird weather"?
   3. How does the climate affect the daily lives of the people? Give examples.
   4. What is the connection between Chukotka and Chelsea Football Club?
   5. How has the lifestyle of the inhabitants changed since Roman Abramovich became governor?
   6. What do the people find difficult to understand?
   7. What does Abramovich own that shows his extreme wealth?
   8. Why does he say he is interested in Chukotka? What do some people suspect?

What do you think?

Discuss in groups.

- Why do you think people live in a place like Chukotka? What would you find most difficult there?
- What do you think the lives of the people were like *before* Abramovich became governor?
- Imagine a year in the life of Roman Abramovich. What do you think is a typical year for him?
- Most people take vacations in warm countries. Are there any cold places in the world you have visited or would like to visit? Where and why?

THE COLDEST

Welcome to CHUKOTKA, where it's currently -30°C and so windy that in the capital, Anadyr, ropes are tied along the streets to stop its inhabitants from blowing away.

It's so cold here that people don't use freezers. They hang their meat in plastic bags on nails above their windows. Spring and summer, when they arrive in June, last a mere eight weeks. The Bering Sea, one of four seas that wash against Chukotkan shores, freezes hard enough to support weights of up to 35 tons. There's no crime because it's just "too darn cold!"

Where yesterday collides with today

Chukotka is, in fact, a remote territory of Russia. It covers 284,000 square miles of frozen landscape, bordering the Bering Strait and straddling the Arctic Circle. Nine time zones ahead of Moscow, it lies right behind the International Dateline, where yesterday collides with today. There is nowhere else on earth earlier than here. Conditions are cruel, and there may seem little to be passionate about other than reindeer, vodka, and the weird weather, but Chukotka has captured the interest of one of the world's richest men, the oil billionaire Roman Abramovich.

From hospitals and theaters to supermarkets

Roman Abramovich

Roman Abramovich, whose fortune is in excess of $14 billion, is the world's 22nd-richest person, and four years ago he was voted governor of Chukotka. Since then, he has been pouring money into this frozen province. Despite not having been born or raised in Chukotka, he has spent an estimated $300 million of his personal fortune on the region. In Anadyr alone he has rebuilt the hospital, dental clinic, and primary school, modernized the airport, opened its first supermarket and movie theater, and sent 8,500 local children on free vacations. He even owns the local radio station, the aptly named Blizzard FM. Abramovich not only owns a radio station, he also owns a soccer team, but not in Chukotka, where it's too cold to play soccer. The team he owns is over 5,000 miles away in London, England, where, in 2003, he bought Chelsea Football Club.

(& EARLIEST!) PLACE ON EARTH

–42°C and falling

The inhabitants of Chelsea, England, could not imagine the life of the inhabitants of Chukotka. Locals like to boast that last winter the wind chill took the recorded temperature of −42°C down to −100°C. Schools were closed for a month. It's generally too cold for outdoor sports or any kind of cafe society, but there are some restaurants and a bar in the supermarket. Snow covers the ground from September to May, which means there are no gardens or woodland: the only flowers are the plastic ones which adorn restaurant tables. But for all this, Abramovich has made Anadyr into a boomtown. People find it difficult to understand what he has done and why he has done it.

From reindeer meat to French camembert

Roman Badanov, news editor of Chukotka TV, says: "Anything Abramovich does is news here because so little happens. Why did he choose us? No one knows—it's a secret he keeps to himself." But he did choose them and they are grateful. In the supermarket you can buy everything from carved walrus tusks to French camembert, Greek olive oil, and Scottish whisky. A few years ago there was only frozen reindeer meat, often eaten for breakfast, lunch, and dinner. And Abramovich takes his duties as a governor seriously—he flies in most months on board his private Boeing 767. He has a built a Canadian-style wooden house, thereby earning himself the unique distinction of owning homes in St. Tropez, Knightsbridge (London), Moscow, and Anadyr. Far from being resentful that he visits only monthly, the local people are astonished that he comes at all. Such is his popularity that the locals refer to BA and AA: Before Abramovich and After Abramovich.

"Why doesn't anyone believe I find this place interesting?"

Abramovich himself asks: "Why doesn't anyone believe I find this place interesting? I think I can change things here—after all, I have achieved success in business." But some suspect that he's hoping for vast returns on Chukotka's natural resources, which include 1.2 billion tons of oil and gas and the second-largest gold reserves in Russia. But his motives don't trouble most of the 73,000 inhabitants. Just one person, Nathalia, who runs the local Internet service, sounded a note of caution: "The people are fools because one day Abramovich will go. This is our moment, but it is only a moment."

VOCABULARY AND PRONUNCIATION
Adverb collocations

Extreme adjectives

Work with a partner.

1 Look at the adjectives in the box. Find some with similar meanings.

> good   bad   marvelous   huge   nice
> wet   clever   enormous   fabulous
> excited   surprised   valuable   small   silly
> funny   interesting   thrilled   delighted
> priceless   amazed   tiny   hilarious
> wonderful   fantastic   ridiculous   awful
> brilliant   pleased   fascinating   gorgeous
> big   soaking   excellent   beautiful

Which adjectives go with which of these adverbs? Why?

very   **absolutely**

2 Complete the conversations with suitable adverbs and adjectives from Exercise 1. Practice them with your partner.

1. **A** Did you get very cold in that snowstorm?
   B Snowstorm! It was a blizzard. We're … !

2. **A** I bet you were pretty excited when your team won.
   B Excited! We were … !

3. **A** I thought she looked kind of silly in that flowery hat, didn't you?
   B Silly! She looked … !

4. **A** Come on, nobody'll notice that tiny pimple on your nose.
   B They will, I just know they will! It's … !

5. **A** I thought the last episode of *Friends* was absolutely hilarious.
   B Mmm. I wouldn't say that. It was … but not hilarious.

6. **A** Len left early. He wasn't feeling well.
   B I'm not surprised. When I saw him this morning he looked … !

3 **T 8.9** Listen and check. Practice again. Make similar conversations with your partner. You could talk about movies, people you know, the weather …

Pretty

4 **T 8.10** The adverb *pretty* has different meanings. Listen and repeat these sentences. Which in each pair is more positive?

1. a. She's pretty smart.
   b. She's pretty smart.
2. a. He's pretty nice.
   b. He's pretty nice.

5 Read these sentences aloud according to the meaning.
1. The movie was pretty interesting. You really should go and see it.
2. The movie was pretty interesting, but I wouldn't recommend it.
3. I'm pretty tired after that last game. Should we call it a day?
4. I'm pretty tired, but I'm up for another game if you are.

T 8.11 Listen, check, and repeat.

A night at the Oscars

6 Read the speech. Who is speaking? Why? Rewrite the speech and make it sound more extreme by changing and adding adjectives and adverbs.

> "I am very surprised and pleased to receive this award. I am grateful to all those nice people who voted for me. *Red Hot in the Snow* was a good movie to act in, not only because of all the smart people involved in the making of it, but also because of the beautiful, exciting, and often pretty dangerous locations in Alaska. None of us could have predicted that it would be such a big success. My special thanks go to Marius Aherne, my director; Lulu Lovelace, my costar; Roger Sims, for writing a script that was both interesting and funny; and last but not least to my wife, Glynis, for her valuable support. I love you all."

7 **T 8.12** Listen and compare your choices.

EVERYDAY ENGLISH
The world around you

1 Look at the signs. Where could you … ?
   - … borrow money to buy a house?
   - … buy a hammer, a screwdriver, and some glue?
   - … go to exercise?
   - … get rid of your newspapers and bottles?
   - … get an inexpensive bed for the night?
   - … get help if you have car trouble?
   - … change your appearance?
   - … replace some of the parts on your car?

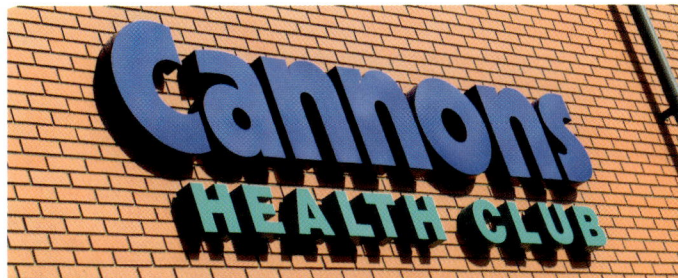

2 **T 8.13** Listen to five conversations. Where are they taking place?

3 In pairs, write similar conversations that take place in two or three of the other places. Read them out to the rest of the class. Where are they taking place?

▶▶ **WRITING** Describing places—My favorite part of town *p. 121*

9 Friends forever

Expressing habit • used to do/doing • Homonyms/Homophones • Making your point

TEST YOUR GRAMMAR

1 Match a line in **A** with a line in **B**.
  Underline the words that express habit.
  Which are past and which are present?

2 Choose the correct ending for these sentences.

| He used to work hard | because he's a mover. |
| He's used to hard work | but now he's retired. |

A	B
1. A reliable friend	my Dad would read me a story at bedtime.
2. In the 1960s, hippies	are always talking about themselves.
3. I think my sister's in love.	will never let you down.
4. When I was a kid	She'll spend hours staring into space.
5. My first girlfriend was Alice.	used to wear flowers in their hair.
6. Bigheaded people	We used to go to the movies on a Friday, and then we'd go for a pizza afterwards.

FRIENDS REUNITED
Expressing habit—used to do/doing

1 One of the most popular websites in the US is Classmates.com. What sort of website do you think it is? Is there a similar website in your country?

2 Read the e-mail from Alison to an old friend from school. Complete it with the lines a–l.

a. used to sit	g. went
b. 'd get	h. was
c. got	i. used to call
d. 's always talking	j. used to calling
e. ~~used to go~~	k. were always giggling
f. 'd go	l. 'll always end up

T 9.1 Listen and check.

3 Which actions in the e-mail happened again and again? Which only happened once?

Classmates.com

From: Alison Wright <AliWright72@yoohoo.com>
Date: Mon, Sep17 6.36 PM
To: sallydavis@yoohoo.com
Subject: Springfield East

Dear Sally,

I'm sending this through classmates.com. Do you remember me? We 1 _e_____ to Springfield East together. You were the first person I 2_____ to know when I started there.

We 3_____ next to each other in class, but then the teachers made us sit apart because we 4_____ so much.

I remember we 5_____ back to your house after school every day and listen to music for hours on end. We 6_____ all the Beatles records as soon as they came out. Once we ate all the food in your fridge and your mother 7_____ furious.

Do you remember that time we nearly blew up the science lab? The teacher 8_____ crazy, but it wasn't our fault. We 9_____ him "Mickey Mouse" because he had sticky-out ears.

I still see Penny, and she's still as wild as ever. We meet up every now and then, and we 10_____ chatting about old times together. She 11_____ about a class reunion. So if you're interested, drop me a line. Looking forward to hearing from you.

Your old friend,

Alison Wright

PS I'm not 12_____ you Sally Davis! To me, you're still Sally Wilkinson!

4 Look at these two sentences.

> We used to go to school together ...
> We'd go back to your house ...

Which sentence is more factual?
Which is more nostalgic?

5 Match a line in **A** with a line in **B**. Practice saying them. Pay attention to contracted forms and weak forms.

A	B
we used to go	him "Mickey Mouse"
we used to sit	to school together
we were always giggling	you Sally Davis
we'd go back	so much
we used to call	to your house
I'm not used to calling	next to each other

T 9.2 Listen and check.

> ### GRAMMAR SPOT
>
> 1 Look at the sentences that express present habit.
>   a. *My sister **works** in a bank.*
>   b. *She**'s always borrowing** my clothes without asking me.*
>   c. *She**'ll go out** on a Friday night and **won't be back** till morning.*
>   Which sentence expresses ...
>   - my attitude to this habit of hers? (I find it annoying.)
>   - a simple fact about her?
>   - characteristic behavior? (This is typical of her.)
>
> 2 Put sentences a–c into the past. Express sentence a in two ways.
>
> 3 Look at these sentences.
>   a. *I've lived next to the airport for years, so I**'m used to** the noise.*
>   b. *I **used to** live in Rome, but now I live in Paris.*
>   c. *I**'m getting used to** traveling on the Metro.*
>   In which sentence is *used* a verb? In which is *used* an adjective?
>   Which sentence expresses ...
>   - a past habit now finished?
>   - a situation which is familiar and no longer strange?
>   - a situation which is still strange but becoming easier?
>
> ▶▶ Grammar Reference 9.1 p. 152

PRACTICE

What's she like?

1 Choose an adjective from the box to describe the people in the sentences.

| easygoing | clumsy | stingy | absentminded |
| argumentative | sensitive | sensible | stubborn |

1. He's always losing things or forgetting where he's put things.
2. She'll always cry at the end of a sad movie.
3. Nothing ever upsets her, or annoys her, or worries her.
4. I'm always dropping things or bumping into things.
5. She's ruled by her head, not her heart. She'll always think things through before she acts.
6. He just won't listen to anyone else's suggestions.
7. I remember that guy Dave. He'd never help pay for gas.
8. And he'd pick a fight with anyone about anything.

2 Add similar sentences to support these statements.

1. My roommate is the messiest person in the whole world.
   He'll leave his dirty clothes everywhere.
2. My boyfriend is insanely jealous.
3. Marc is just the coolest guy I know.
4. My mother really gets on my nerves.
5. But my grandma was so sweet.
6. My dog Bruno was my best friend.
7. Your problem is you're self-centered.
8. My sister's so nosy.

Discussing grammar

3 In pairs, decide which line in **B** best continues the line in **A**.

A	B
1. My friend Joe buys and sells cars. 2. He's always buying new things for himself—a DVD, a laptop. 3. He'll buy a shirt and only wear it once.	He's a real techno-geek. Don't you think that's wasteful of him? He earns tons of money.
4. When I was young, we used to take vacations by the seaside. 5. My dad and I would build sandcastles and go swimming together. 6. One year we went to East Africa.	What an adventure that was! We'd go to the same place year after year. I remember those days with such fondness!
7. John usually does the cooking 8. He used to do the cooking 9. He's used to doing the cooking 10. He's getting used to doing the cooking	because he's been doing it for years. but he still burns things. Maybe one day he'll get it. but then he stopped. but he isn't tonight. I am.

Parents

4 **T 9.3** Listen to four people talking about their relationship with their parents. Is/Was it a good relationship?

5 **T 9.3** Listen again. These lines are similar to what they say. What are their actual words?

1. ... she talked to me very openly ...
   ... we used to go out shopping ...
2. My wife always asks me questions ...
   ... we didn't talk very much ...
   ... every week he took me to the barber.
3. ... she always tells me to pick things up ...
   She goes on for hours ...
4. We did a lot together as a family.
   ... he brought us each a treat ...

6 Write a few sentences about the relationship between you and your parents. Tell your partner about it.

Answering questions

7 Answer the questions with a form of *used to*.

1. **A** You don't like your new teacher, do you?
   B Not a lot, but we're getting used to her .
2. **A** How can you get up at five o'clock in the morning?
   B No problem. I 'm used to it .
3. **A** How come you know Mexico City so well?
   B I _____ live there.
4. **A** How are you finding your new job?
   B Difficult, but I _____ it bit by bit.
5. **A** Do you read comics?
   B I _____ when I was young, but not anymore.
6. **A** You two argue so much. How can you live together?
   B After 20 years of marriage we _____ each other.

T 9.4 Listen and check.

76 Unit 9 • Friends forever

LISTENING AND SPEAKING
A teacher I'll never forget

1 Look at the pictures. What are the teachers doing? What are the students doing? How have teaching styles changed over the years?

"That's an interesting question Timmy. I suggest you ask your search engine."

2 **T 9.5** Listen to four people talking about a teacher they'll never forget. What characteristics of a good and a bad teacher do they mention?

3 Discuss the questions.
1. Why did Alan like his teacher? What are some of the things he'd do?
2. Why didn't John like his teacher? What are some of the things he used to do?
3. What does Liz say about her teacher? What will she never forget?
4. Why does Kate have two opposing views of Mr. Brown?
5. What comments do they all make about their teacher's name?

What do you think?
Who is a teacher you'll never forget? Why? What was/is she/he like?

> **SPOKEN ENGLISH** Adjective intensifiers
>
> Look at these lines from the tapescript.
>
> All the kids were **scared stiff** of him.
> … your answer was **dead wrong**.
>
> These are compounds that intensify the meaning of the adjective.
>
> Complete the sentences with a word from the box.
>
> brand   stiff   freezing   tiny   wide   great   boiling   fast
>
> 1. They live in this _____ big house in the center of London.
> 2. I made one _____ little mistake on my driver's test, but I still failed.
> 3. Careful with the soup—it's _____ hot. Don't burn yourself.
> 4. It's _____ cold in here. Can't we turn up the heat?
> 5. Do you like my car? It's _____ new.
> 6. Don't worry. You won't wake the children. They're _____ asleep.
> 7. I take a cold shower every morning. After that I feel _____ awake.
> 8. "I'm fed up with this class." "Me, too. I'm bored _____."

Unit 9 · Friends forever 77

READING AND SPEAKING
Friends past

1 Discuss the questions.
   1. What are these kinds of TV programs like?

   | soap opera | sitcom | game show |
   | documentary | reality TV | current affairs |

   Think of examples of each in your country. What are your favorites?
   2. What American programs are on TV in your country? Do you watch any of them?

2 **T 9.6** Listen to the theme song to *Friends*, one of the most successful American sitcoms ever. Can you remember any of the lines?

3 What do you know about *Friends*? Why do you think it was so successful?

4 Read the first half of the article and answer the questions.
   1. What line in paragraph 1 summarizes the stories in *Friends*?
   2. How long did the series last?
   3. Why, according to Steve Beverly, was the show so popular?
   4. What is so enviable about the characters' lifestyle?
   5. How did *Friends* capture the spirit of the times? Give two examples of how it defined it.
   6. Why did *Friends* become more popular after 9/11?
   7. How did the series change people's language, hair, and drinking habits?

5 Read the second half of the article.
   1. Who is related to who? Who is in love with who? What is the mixed emotion described at the end of the article?
   2. What is each character like? Find some examples of their behavior that illustrate the kind of person they are.

6 **T 9.7** Listen to people describing a character in *Friends* without saying who it is. Which character is being described?

Language work

Match a word from the first part of the text in **A** with a similar word in **B**.

A	B
the small screen	looked for
trials	met
trendy	feeling deep sadness
encountered	difficulties
grieving	television
sought	fashionable

What do you think?

- Who is your favorite TV character? Why?
- Describe one of your closest friends.

IT WAS THE AMERICAN SITCOM THAT DEFINED A GENERATION—and introduced one of the world's most famous haircuts. The six stars of *Friends*, among the longest-running, most successful series ever to hit the small screen, went their separate ways after 237 episodes and a decade together as roommates, sharing the trials of their lives, loves, and careers in a trendy New York apartment. The last episode was seen by an estimated world audience of over 100 million viewers.

"*Friends* had a huge influence on American TV history," said Steve Beverly, professor of communication arts. "This group of six reflected a microcosm of what people their age encountered in their daily lives. Viewers related to them. We *all* wanted a life like theirs—the cool New York apartment with foosball and easy chairs, and the social circle of beautiful, supportive friends."

We also wanted to drink endless cappuccinos. Interestingly enough, the first New York Starbucks store opened in the same year that *Friends* started. The dual rise of coffee culture and *Friends* was one example of how the show captured the spirit of the times. At other times it defined it. The "Rachel" haircut was copied by millions of women.

The series has even been credited with influencing how many of us speak. Researchers analyzed every episode to explore whether popular culture influenced how we speak. Prior to the series, the most common way to intensify an adjective was by using *very* or *really*. On *Friends*, the most common intensifier was *so*. "This guy is like so cool," they said, and now we all say.

The show enjoyed a huge surge in ratings after the September 11th terrorist attacks, as grieving Americans struggled to make sense of the real horrors that had unfolded around them. In the familiar comforts of the show, they sought the return of a feel-good factor, according to Robert Thompson, professor of television and popular culture. "*Friends* is set not in the real New York, but in the New York of some fantasy where the rooms in the apartments are huge, everybody leaves their doors unlocked and people don't fly planes into buildings," he said.

F·R·I·E·N·D·S PAST

It was much more than a brilliant comedy, says **Claire Rooney**—it changed our language, our hair, and even our drinking habits

So who are these characters?

Ross has been in love with Rachel, the best friend of his sister Monica, since childhood, and throughout the whole series they have an on-off romance. In the final episode they actually do get back together again. Ross is a bit of a bore and a geek. He's always whining.

Chandler, a computer programmer, used to share an apartment with Joey. He's constantly telling jokes and making everybody laugh. He had a few relationships throughout the series, mostly disastrous because he would always find flaws in the women he dated, but then married Monica.

Joey is a New Yorker with Italian roots. He's an actor who manages to spend most of the series unemployed. Nevertheless he has total belief in his talents. He's rather dense, but lovable and charming. He'll cheer himself up with food or women.

Rachel is a spoiled little rich girl who gets a job in the local coffee shop and later becomes a fashion consultant. She is terrible in a crisis and will throw her arms up in despair. Rachel and Ross get together so many times, but things keep going wrong, until they finally make it permanent in the last episode.

Phoebe is the group hippie. She is wild and very eccentric, and she's always smiling. She is a spiritual masseuse who is always communicating with the dead and chanting about auras. She is best known for her unique guitar playing—her most famous song is "Smelly Cat."

Monica, believe it or not, used to be fat. She is a deeply insecure character and is always cleaning the house. She's also bossy and has to have her own way. Her desire is to find her dream man, get married, and have babies. Eventually she settles down with Chandler.

More like a way of life

Friends is more than just a sitcom. It's a way of life. Our attitudes to the characters' lives is a mixture of envy—"How do they get to sit on sofas all day sipping coffee and being witty?"—and disdain: "Don't they have anything better to do with their time, like earn a living to pay for that Manhattan apartment?"

They were supposed to be in their midtwenties, with lives untroubled by work and responsibility. With the cast approaching 40, the show had to come to an end. But of course, *Friends* will last forever.

Unit 9 • Friends forever

VOCABULARY AND PRONUNCIATION
Homonyms and homophones

1. Work on your own. What do these words mean?

   | fine   match   park   book   cross   mean |

2. **T 9.8** Write down the words you hear.

3. Work with a partner. Compare your answers to Exercises 1 and 2. Do you have any differences? What are they?

Homonyms

4. Homonyms are words with the same spelling and more than one meaning.

   > a **bank** on Main Street
   > the **bank** of a river
   > I've supported you up till now, but don't **bank** on it forever.

   Complete the pairs of sentences with the same word used twice.

   1. You'll like Paul. He's a really _____ guy. Easygoing and very good looking.
      There was a lovely _____ breeze coming off the sea.
   2. "What's today's _____?" "The third."
      I've got a _____ tonight. I'm going out with Carol.
   3. *Friends* is _____ in New York.
      My wife bought me a chess _____ for my birthday.
   4. He goes to the gym every day. He's very _____.
      The pants are too small. They don't _____ you.
   5. I can't _____ people who never stop talking about themselves.
      My four-year-old son won't go anywhere without his teddy _____.

5. Think of two meanings for these words.

   | wave   suit   fan   miss   type |
   | point   train   right   mind   fair |

Homophones

6. Homophones are words with the same pronunciation, but different spellings and different meanings.

   > the **road** to the town center
   > She **rode** a horse.
   > I **rowed** across the river.

   Write in the correct word.

   1. hole/whole — the _____ world
      a _____ in the ground
   2. piece/peace — a _____ of cake
      war and _____
   3. flour/flower — a rose is a _____
      _____ to make bread
   4. sale/sail — a yacht has a _____
      buy clothes on _____
   5. sell/cell — salespeople _____ things
      a prisoner lives in a _____

7. Think of a homophone for these words.

   | bored   war   hire   pair   plain   waist   seas   aloud |

8. **T 9.9** A lot of children's jokes are made with homonyms and homophones. Here are two! Which word makes the joke?

A How do you keep cool at a football game?
B I don't know.
A Sit next to a fan.

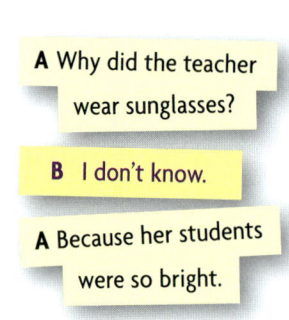

A Why did the teacher wear sunglasses?
B I don't know.
A Because her students were so bright.

T 9.10 Listen to some more jokes. Which word makes the joke? Practice telling them to each other.

EVERYDAY ENGLISH
Making your point

1 **T 9.11** Listen to Vicky, Al, and Beth-Anne talking about whether people should pay more tax on fast food. Who is for it, who is against it, and who is undecided?

2 Match a line in **A** with a line in **B** as they appear in the tapescript on page 137.

A	B
If you	is that …
Another thing	the point.
That's not	I understand it …
The point	you the truth …
To tell	my opinion …
I suppose	worries me is that …
As far as	I'm trying to make is that …
Anyway, as I	point is that …
If you want	the problem is that …
As	was saying …
But the main	I'm concerned …
What really	ask me …

T 9.12 Check your answers. Listen carefully and practice the lines.

> **Music of English** ♪
> Notice the stress patterns in the expressions for making your point. It's important that you get the stress pattern right if you want to make your point effectively.

3 Write the adverbs that end in *-ly* in tapescript 9.11.

firstly   secondly   personally

4 Match a line in **A** with a line in **B**.

A	B
1. First of all,	there are problems with the cost.
2. In addition to **this**,	I'd like to **give** my conclusion.
3. Finally,	I'd like to **look** at the **general** problem.
4. In my opinion,	how do you educate people to have a better diet?
5. Generally speaking,	fast food should be totally banned.
6. The problem is,	as a nation we don't get enough exercise.
7. As far as I know,	I don't know the answer to this problem.
8. To be exact,	there are five others like this.
9. To be honest,	this problem is quite common.

5 Have a class debate. Choose a topic you feel strongly about, something local to your situation perhaps, or one from this list.

- Being vegetarian
- Diets for children
- The effects of tourism
- Experiments on animals

Divide into groups to prepare your ideas. When you're ready, conduct the debate.

▶▶ **WRITING** Writing for talking—What I want to talk about is … *p. 122*

Unit 9 • Friends forever   81

10 Risking life and limb

Modal auxiliary verbs 2 • Synonyms • Metaphors and idioms—the body

▶ **TEST YOUR GRAMMAR**

1 All modal verbs can be used to express degrees of probability. Which of these sentences do this? Put a (✓). Which don't? Put a (✗).

1. She must be very rich. ✓
2. I must do my homework. ✗
3. I can't sleep because of the noise.
4. They can't be in. There are no lights on.
5. I think that's Jane but I might be wrong.
6. You should see a doctor.
7. I could swim when I was five.
8. Cheer up! Things could be worse.
9. The train may be late due to bad weather.
10. May I make a suggestion?

2 Put sentences 1–6 in the past.

T 10.1 Listen and check.

ÖTZI THE ICEMAN
Modal auxiliary verbs in the past

1 The body of a 5,300-year-old man was discovered in the Italian Alps in 1991. It had been preserved in ice. He was named Ötzi after the Ötz Valley, where he was found. Look at the pictures.

What do you think …

   … he was?
   … he wore?
   … he ate?

Where did he live?
How did he die?
How old was he when he died?

> He was probably a hunter.
> He could have been a warrior.

2 **T 10.2** Listen to two people, Alan and Bill, discussing the questions in Exercise 1. Give one of their answers to each question.

82 Unit 10 • Risking life and limb

3 Answer these questions about Ötzi using the words in *italics*.

1. What was he?
   a hunter/shepherd   *could*
2. What was he doing in the mountains?
   looking after his sheep/gotten lost   *might*
3. Where did he live? What did he wear?
   a cave   animal skins   *must*
4. How did he die?
   asleep/cold and starvation   *may*
5. Was it a good idea to go so high?
   so high on his own   *shouldn't*
   protective clothing   *should*
6. What did he eat?
   a lot of meat and berries   *must*
   crops like grains to make bread   *might can't*
   meat   *'d have thought*
7. Did they travel much?
   (not) much at all   *wouldn't have thought*
   stayed in the same area   *must*
8. How old was he when he died?
   between 40 and 45   *could*
   pretty old in those days   *must*

4 **T 10.3** Listen and check. Practice the sentences, paying attention to contracted forms and weak forms.

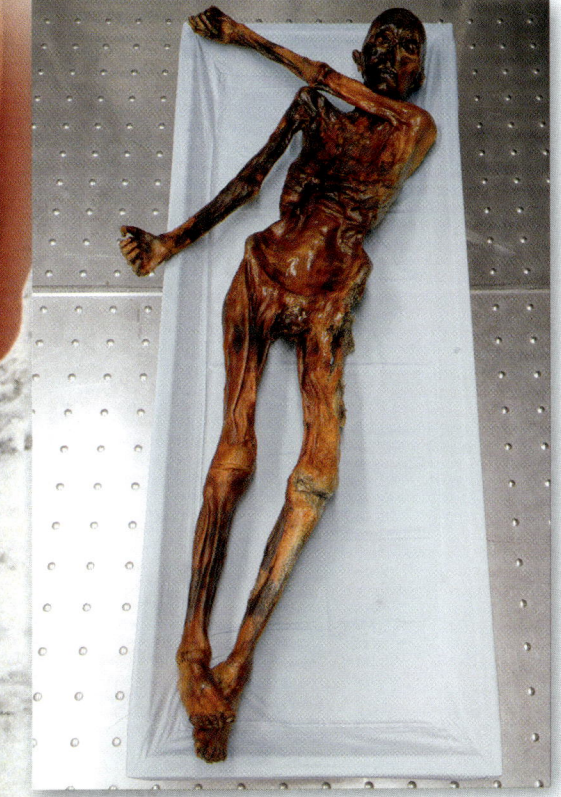

5 Here are some more things found on or near Ötzi's body. How can you explain them?

I bet he used it to …
That must have/might have/could have been for …
I think/guess …
I'd have thought …
I wouldn't have thought …

6 Read the results of recent tests done on Ötzi on page 110. Were Alan and Bill right or wrong in their assumptions? Were *you* right in *your* assumptions?

GRAMMAR SPOT

1 Write *certain* or *possible* next to these modal auxiliary verbs according to the degree of probability they express.

They must have		
They might have They could have They may have	arrived.	
They can't have		

2 What concept do these modal verbs express? Choose a definition on the right.

You shouldn't have told a lie. | This was possible but it
You idiot! You could have killed | didn't happen.
   yourself! | You did this but it was wrong.

▶▶ Grammar Reference 10.1 pp. 152–153

Unit 10 · Risking life and limb   83

PRACTICE

Discussing grammar

1 Underline the correct answer.

1. Sorry I'm late. I *should have gone/had to go* to the post office.
2. I looked for Pearl but I *couldn't find/couldn't have found* her.
3. I don't know where Paul is. He *had to go/must have gone* home early.
4. I *had to work/must have worked* hard when I was in school.
5. You *can't have said/shouldn't have said* anything to Pam about her birthday party. It was going to be a surprise.
6. You *shouldn't have bought/couldn't have bought* a new vacuum cleaner. I managed to fix the old one.
7. You *should have asked/must have asked* me earlier. I *might have given/would have given* you a ride.
8. You *can't have done/shouldn't have done* your homework already! You only started five minutes ago.
9. You *could have told/must have told* me class had been cancelled! If you had, I *shouldn't have gotten/wouldn't have gotten* up so early.
10. You were lucky to get out of the car unhurt. You *would have been/could have been* badly injured.

2 Complete the sentences with a modal verb in the past.

1. I *did* tell you about Joe's party. You **must not have** been listening.
2. Thanks so much for all your help. I _____ managed without you.
3. Flowers, for me! Oh, that's so kind, but you really _____ .
4. Come on! We're only five minutes late. The movie _____ started yet.
5. I don't believe that Kathy's going out with Mark. She _____ told me, I know she would.
6. We raced to get to the airport on time, but we _____ worried. The flight was delayed.
7. We've got a letter here that isn't for us. The mailman _____ delivered it by mistake.
8. You _____ gone swimming in such rough seas. You _____ drowned!

T 10.4 Listen and check. Practice the sentences with a partner.

Making assumptions

3 **T 10.5** You will hear one half of a telephone conversation. Who are the people? What are they talking about? Make assumptions.

They must be divorced.   *They might just be separated.*

4 Work with a partner. Look at the tapescript on page 138. Write what you think is the other half of the conversation. Compare with other students.

5 **T 10.6** Do the same with the second conversation.

SPOKEN ENGLISH Expressions with modals

There are many fixed expressions with modal auxiliary verbs often found in spoken English. Match a line in **A** with a line in **B**.

A	B
1. "That exam was totally impossible!"	a. "Sorry! I thought you knew."
2. "You might as well apply for the job, even though you're too young."	b. "You can say that again!"
3. I know I shouldn't have eaten a whole tub of ice cream …	c. but I just couldn't help it.
4. "I'm going to tell her exactly what I think of her."	d. "Yes, why not! After all, I've got nothing to lose."
5. "You should have told me that Jackie and Dave broke up!"	e. "I wouldn't do that if I were you."
6. "I think you should forget all about her and move on."	f. "Me, too. I'm dying for some coffee."
7. "You should have been here yesterday! You'd have died laughing!"	g. "Believe me, I would if I could."
8. "Then I found out that Annie's been going out with … guess who? Dave!"	h. "Why? What was so funny?"
9. I'd known this guy for five minutes when he asked me to marry him!	i. "Duh! I could have told you *that*."
10. "I could use a break."	j. I just couldn't believe it!

T 10.7 Listen and check. What extra lines do you hear? What are the contexts? Practice the conversations with a partner.

SPEAKING
It all went wrong!

6 Write some notes about an occasion in your life when everything went wrong. Tell the class. They can comment and ask questions.

▶▶ **WRITING** Formal and informal letters and e-mails—Do's and don'ts *p. 123*

READING AND SPEAKING
Go west, young man!

1 Do you know any movies about cowboys and Indians? What is a typical plot? Who are the "good guys" and who are the "bad guys"? Do you have a favorite western?

2 You are going to read about the American West in the 1800s, when there were conflicts over land between white settlers and Native Americans. In what other countries have settlers taken the lands of native inhabitants? What has happened there?

Unit 10 • Risking life and limb   85

Reading

3 What do you understand by the title of the article? Look at the six headings. Make guesses about the contents of the paragraphs.

4 Read the first two sections. Answer the questions.
1. Why did the white settlers want to head west? (There are several reasons.)
2. What were some of the natural dangers to overcome? What could go wrong? What accidents could have been avoided?
3. What do these numbers refer to?

| 1843 | 14,000 | 2,000 | 4½ | 15 | 25 |

5 Read about the Donner party. Complete the sentences using the verb in parentheses and a modal verb.

1. They _____ (set out) so late in the year.
2. They _____ (follow) an established route.
3. They _____ (spend) the winter in the mountains.
4. They _____ (take) enough food.
5. They _____ (be) really starving to do what they did.

6 Read the rest of the article. Answer the questions.
1. Describe the early relationship between the settlers and Native Americans. What was the main reason why it changed?
2. Describe the Native Americans' culture. Over what issues were they bound to clash with the settlers?
3. How did the white people help the Native Americans? How did they exploit them?
4. How did the war finally end?
5. Find different ways the text refers to the white people and the Native Americans.

What do you think?

- Do you think native inhabitants of today should receive financial compensation for the land that was taken from their ancestors?
- What are the arguments for and against developing remote parts of the world such as rainforests, deserts, and Antarctica?

GO WEST,

THE WESTERN MIGRATION

The American West covers a vast area from the Mississippi River to the Pacific coast. Until the early 19th century, few white settlers had explored it. In the following decades, however, more than 500,000 Americans moved there from the eastern United States. Land for farming was scarce in the East, and the US government promised these pioneers land in the newly-acquired states of California and Oregon. Others came in search of gold or adventure, or to practice their own form of religion. Some even believed it was their patriotic duty to claim the land from the Native Americans who were already living there.

THE HAZARDOUS JOURNEY

Large-scale migration began in 1843. By 1848, over 14,000 settlers had followed. Much of the land they crossed consisted of mountains, deserts, and huge, treeless plains. To avoid the worst of the winter blizzards in the mountains, travelers normally began their journey in late April or early May. It was not possible to travel earlier in the year, as there was not enough grass on the Great Plains to feed the livestock. If everything went according to plan, the 2,000-mile journey took around four and a half months, covering about 15 miles a day. Any delay meant that fierce snowstorms would be encountered in the Sierra Nevada mountains. Migrants suffered from disease, violent dust storms, wagons stuck in mud, and plagues of insects such as mosquitoes. One in 25 of the migrants failed to make their destination. Many deaths were self-inflicted. Not experienced in the use of guns, they frequently shot themselves or each other by mistake.

YOUNG MAN!

The 2,000-mile journey took four and a half months.

THE TRAGEDY OF THE DONNER PARTY

In 1846, a group from Illinois, including the Donner family, decided to emigrate to California. Their story was to become one of the best-known tragedies in the history of Western emigration. They made two crucial mistakes. They started late, and followed an untested route and got lost. Morale became poor, tempers flared, and one of the men was stabbed to death. It was late October by the time they started to climb the Sierra Nevada mountains, and they were desperately short of food. Snow made the mountains impassable. They prepared to spend the winter in the mountain snow. Starving, they ate glue, fur, and dogs. Eventually, they ate their own dead. Out of 81 travelers, over half died.

FIRST CONTACTS WITH NATIVE AMERICANS

When the white people first explored the American West, they found Native Americans living in every part of the region, many of them on the Great Plains. Each tribe had its own complex culture and social structure. They didn't believe that land should be owned by individuals or families, but should belong to all people. They believed that human beings were indivisible from all the other elements of the natural world: animals, birds, soil, air, mountains, water, and the sun. In the early days of migration, relations between the pioneers and Native Americans were generally friendly. Trade was common, and sometimes fur traders married and integrated into Indian society. The travelers gave Native Americans blankets, beads, and mirrors in exchange for food. They also sold them guns and ammunition. In the 1840s, attacks on wagons were rare and the Plains Indians generally regarded these first white travelers with amusement.

GOLD FEVER AND CONFLICT

Then, in 1849, came an event which greatly changed the relationship between settlers and Native Americans—the Gold Rush. Thousands of men of many different nationalities flocked to California, and later to Colorado and Nevada, to search for gold. With the rush came the development of mining camps and the growth of industries, towns, shops, road systems, and railroads. Much of this took place on sacred Native American hunting grounds. Inevitably, conflict ensued. To the settlers, the West was a wilderness waiting to be tamed, and a potential source of profit. Most did not realize the damage they were doing to the environment. Native Americans did little farming and mining. They were hunters, and central to their way of life was the wild buffalo. There had been enormous herds of buffalo, estimated at 60 million, but by the mid-1880s they were virtually extinct, having been hunted by white Americans.

THE FINAL BATTLE

The US government took over more and more Indian land. Native Americans were persuaded—sometimes forced—to live in reservations far from their homelands. Tensions finally exploded into war in the 1860s. Terrible atrocities were committed by both sides. Finally, in 1890, the Seventh Cavalry surrounded a band of Sioux at Wounded Creek and killed 146 men, women and children. The war was over.

LISTENING AND VOCABULARY
Synonyms—the story of Jim and the lion

In 1907 Hilaire Belloc published *Cautionary Tales for Children*. They are humorous verses with a moral.

1 Look at the title of the poem and the pictures. Guess the answers to these questions.
   1. Where did his nurse* take him?
   2. Was Jim a well-behaved little boy who always did what he was told? Or was he naughty?
   3. How far did he get when he ran away?
   4. How did the lion go about eating him?
   5. Who tried to help Jim? Did this work?
   6. How did his parents react?
      *Nowadays we would say *nanny*, not *nurse*.

2 **T 10.8** Listen and check.

3 Complete the lines with a word on the right. Think of style, rhythm, and rhyme. It might help to say the poem out loud. Do the first verse.

4 **T 10.8** Listen and check your answers to the first verse. Then do the same for the rest of the poem.

5 What is the moral of this poem? What is the tone?
   Jim's parents, we are told, were "concerned" about their son. Why is this funny?

What do you think?
- What were your favorite stories as a child? Tell the class about one of them.
- Were they scary? Funny?
- Who were the main characters? Were the stories based on real life or fantasy?
- Did they have a moral? A happy ending?

Jim, who ran away from his nurse, and was eaten by a lion

There was a boy whose name was Jim;
His _____ were very good to him.   buddies / friends
They gave him tea, and cakes, and jam,
And slices of _____ ham,   delicious / tasty
And read him _____ through   novels / stories
   and through,
And even took him to the zoo—
But there it was the _____ fate   dreadful / appalling
Befell him, I now _____.   describe / relate

You know—at least you ought to know,
For I have _____ told you so—   frequently / often
That children never are _____   allowed / permitted
To leave their nurses in a crowd;
Now this was Jim's especial foible,
He ran away when he was able,
And on this _____ day   unlucky / inauspicious
He slipped his hand and _____ away!   hurried / ran

He hadn't gone a yard when—bang!
With open jaws, a lion _____,   sprang / leapt
And hungrily began to eat
The boy: _____ at his feet.   beginning / commencing
Now just _____ how it feels   imagine / guess
When _____ your toes and then   initially / first
   your heels,
And then by gradual degrees,
Your shins and ankles, calves and knees,
Are _____ eaten, bit by bit.   gradually / slowly

No wonder Jim _____ it!   loathed / detested
No wonder that he _____ "Hi!"   shouted / screamed
The honest keeper heard his cry,
Though very _____, he almost ran   fat / overweight
To help the little gentleman.
"Ponto!" he cried, with _____ frown   furious / angry
"Let go, sir! Down, sir! Put it down!"
....
The lion having reached his head,
The _____ boy was dead!   miserable / unfortunate

When nurse _____ his parents they   told / informed
Were more _____ than I can say.   concerned / upset
His mother, as she dried her eyes,
Said, "Well—it gives me no _____,   shock / surprise
He would not do as he was told!"
His father, who was _____   reserved / self-controlled
Bade all the _____ round attend   kids / children
To James' miserable _____,   fate / end
And always keep a-hold of nurse
For fear of finding something worse.

88 Unit 10 • Risking life and limb

EVERYDAY ENGLISH
Metaphors and idioms—the body

1 Complete the sentences with a part of the body.

> Your _____ is associated with intelligence.
> Your _____ are associated with manual skills.
> Your _____ is associated with emotions.

2 In which one of these sentences is the word in *italics* used literally? Rephrase the words used metaphorically.
   1. Can you give me a *hand* with this sofa? It's so heavy.
   2. She's so smart. She's *heading* for great things in life.
   3. But she's not at all *bigheaded*.
   4. We shook *hands* and introduced ourselves.
   5. My daughter has a very good *head* for business.
   6. I'd offer to help, but I've got my *hands* full at the moment.
   7. I know she shouts a lot, but she's really got a *heart* of gold.
   8. We had a *heart-to-heart* talk, and things are much clearer now.
   9. My parents wanted me to be a lawyer, but my *heart* wasn't in it. Now I'm a journalist.

3 Complete the sentences with one of these expressions.

> face the fact   putting a brave face   on its last legs   goes to their head
> pulling your leg   getting back on his feet   a sharp tongue

   1. My car's been driven over 200,000 kilometers. It's _____ now. I'll have to buy a new one.
   2. With so many celebrities, success _____ and they start to believe they're really special.
   3. She's being very courageous and _____ on it, but I know she's in a lot of pain.
   4. He lost everything when his business failed, but he's got a new job now and he's _____.
   5. I'm almost 75. I simply have to _____ that I'm not as young as I was.
   6. "Oh no! I forwarded your e-mail complaining about work to the boss!" "Are you serious?" "No, I'm just _____."
   7. "Sue says some really cruel things." "Yes, she's got _____."

4 **T 10.9** Listen to three conversations. Replace some of the phrases you hear with expressions on this page.

   T 10.10 Listen and check.

5 Look up another part of the body in your dictionary. Find one or two useful idioms or metaphorical uses. Explain them to the rest of the class.

Unit 10 • Risking life and limb 89

11 In your dreams

Hypothesizing • Expressions with *if* • Word pairs • Moans and groans

TEST YOUR GRAMMAR

1 Helen is feeling very sorry for herself. Read column **A**. What are her problems?

2 **T 11.1** Join a line in **A** with a wish in **B**. Listen and check.

3 Write down one thing you're not happy about. Tell the class what you wish.

A		B
1. It's raining again. 2. I'm not going out tonight. 3. There's nothing good on TV. 4. I don't like my job. 5. My boyfriend and I broke up last week. 6. I know he won't call me. 7. I feel really depressed. 8. I can't talk to anyone about it.	I wish	I was. I did. I didn't. I could. he would. there was. it wasn't. we hadn't.

IF ONLY...
Hypothesizing about the past and present

1 Look at the photos. Each one illustrates someone's regret or wish. What do you think the regret or wish is?

2 **T 11.2** Listen to the people talking. Who says what? Number the pictures in the order you hear.

a.

b.

c.

Unit 11 • In your dreams

3 **T 11.2** Listen again and complete the lines. Who is speaking?

1. I shouldn't have …
   If only I hadn't …
   I wouldn't worry …

2. If only we could …
   That would …
   I'd just …
   Sometimes I wish …

3. What would you give … ?
   Which one would you choose if … ?
   … if I won the lottery, I'd …
   I wouldn't—I'd …

4. Don't you wish you … ?
   But *you* could have …

5. I shouldn't have …
   Come on, couldn't you … ?
   Supposing you …

4 Work with a partner. Use the lines in Exercise 3 to help you remember the conversations. Practice them.

5 What are the facts behind some of the wishes and regrets?

I shouldn't have gone out last night.
She did go out last night. She went to a party.

d.

e.

GRAMMAR SPOT

Hypothesizing—past and present

1 All of these sentences are hypothetical. That is, they imagine changing certain facts. What are the facts?
   a. *I wish I **knew** the answer.*   I don't know the answer.
   b. *If only I **could come** to the party.*
   c. *If only I'**d told** the truth.*
   d. *If I **didn't get** so nervous, I'**d get** better results.*
   e. *If you'**d helped** us, we'**d have finished** by now.*
   f. *I **should have listened** to your advice.*
   g. *I wish I **spoke** French well.*
   h. *I wish you **would speak** to him.*

2 Which of the sentences are about present time? Which are about past time?

3 Look at sentences c, d, and e. What are the full forms of the contractions *I'd*, *you'd*, and *we'd*?

4 Other expressions are also used to hypothesize. Complete the sentences with the facts.

   It's time you **knew** the truth. The fact is that you …
   I'd rather you **didn't smoke**. The fact is that you …
   I'd rather they **hadn't come**. The fact is that they …
   Supposing you'**d fallen** and **hurt** yourself! Fortunately, you …

▶▶ Grammar Reference 11.1 p. 153

PRACTICE

1 Express a wish or regret about these facts. Use the words in parentheses.

1. I don't speak English fluently. (*wish*)
   I wish I spoke English fluently.
2. You speak very fast. I don't understand. (*if*)
3. I'm an only child. (*wish*)
4. We don't have enough money to go on vacation. (*if only*)
5. I get up at six o'clock every morning. I have to go to work. (*wouldn't/if*)
6. I didn't learn to ski until I was 40. I'm not very good. (*if*)
7. My 13-year-old sister wants to be older. (*she wishes*)
8. My best friend always borrows my things without asking. (*I'd rather*)
9. I don't know anything about computers. I can't help you. (*if*)
10. We want to take a break. (*it's time*)

Unit 11 • In your dreams   91

Broken dreams

2 Read Sozos's sad story. Explain the title. Complete his final regret.

Politeness doesn't pay!
SOZOS PAPADOPADOS   A RETIRED BOAT BUILDER

IN THE 1970s, Sozos was a newly arrived Greek immigrant in Australia. Each and every week he bought a lottery ticket. One week he was in line to buy a ticket when an old lady stepped into the shop, also wanting to buy one. Sozos, being a polite young man and remembering his mother's words, "always be kind to old people," offered the woman his place in line. The next week, to his shock and horror, he saw on TV that the winning ticket was the one the old lady bought. She had won $6 million.

Sozos says: "I think about it to this day. How different would my life have been if only I … ?"

3 Use these words to form sentences about Sozos.
   1. Sozos shouldn't/allow the old lady/cut in line.
   2. If he/not follow/mother's advice/his life/very different.
   3. If he/contact the old lady/she might/give him/money.
   4. What/happen if he/keep his place/line?

   Answer question 4. Use your imagination.

4 **T 11.3** Listen to **Marty** talking about a vacation he and his ex-wife **Carrie** had in Vanuatu in the South Pacific a few years ago. Work with a partner and complete these sentences about them.
   1. If they'd known that …
   2. They should have …
   3. They shouldn't have …
   4. If they hadn't …
   5. They wish they …

   Compare your answers with the class.

5 Form the question and answer it.
   What/happen/if there/not be/earthquake?

Talking about you

6 What do you wish was different about your life? Make a wish list about some of these things and discuss it with other students.

My wish list
- home
- social life
- money
- family
- work
- relationships
- friends
- vacations

If only I wish	I you he she we they	was/were … wasn't/weren't … did/didn't … had/hadn't … could … would/wouldn't …

SPOKEN ENGLISH Expressions with *if*

There are many fixed expressions with *if* often found in spoken English. Match a line in **A** with one in **B**.

A	B
1. Would it be OK if	if you've got a minute?
2. Win? What do you mean? If you ask me,	I'd never forgive myself.
3. If you knew what I know,	If anything, he's a little shy.
4. Could I have a word with you	I left a little early today?
5. If anything went wrong,	we can always postpone it.
6. If all goes well,	you'd never go out with him again.
7. It was a Thursday, not a Tuesday,	if any.
8. Well, if worst comes to worst,	they don't stand a chance.
9. You haven't made much progress,	we should be finished by Friday.
10. I don't think he's cold or arrogant.	if I remember correctly.

T 11.4 Listen to the conversations and check. What extra lines do you hear? What are the contexts? Practice with a partner.

VOCABULARY AND PRONUNCIATION
Word pairs

> There are many pairs of words joined by a conjunction. The order of the words is fixed.
> 1 Read these sentences aloud.
>   **Each and every week** he bought a ticket.
>   To his **shock and horror** he saw her on TV.
> 2 Complete these well-known ones.
>   Life's full of **ups and** _____.
>   There are always **pros and** _____ in any argument.
>   We'll find out the truth **sooner or** _____.

1 Match a word pair with a definition.

A	B
off and on	compromise/be flexible
wait and see	occasionally
ins and outs	be patient and find out later
give and take	generally speaking
by and large	exact details
grin and bear it	accept it or refuse, I don't care.
odds and ends	tolerate it as best you can
take it or leave it	things

2 Complete the sentences with a word pair from above.
   1. In any relationship you have to be prepared to _____ . You can't have your own way all the time.
   2. I didn't buy much at the mall. Just a few _____ for the kids. Socks for Ben and hairbands for Jane.
   3. I'd been visiting Florida _____ for years before I finally moved there.
   4. It's difficult to explain the _____ of the rules of baseball. It's so complicated.
   5. "What did you get me for my birthday?" "You'll have to _____."
   6. "Oh, no! The Burtons are coming for lunch! I hate their kids!" "I'm sorry, but you'll just have to _____ . It's only for an hour or so."
   7. OK, you can have it for $90. That's my final offer, _____ .
   8. California has lots of faults, of course, but _____ , it's a pleasant place to live.

   T 11.5 Listen and check.

3 Work with a partner. Match a word in **A** with a word in **B** and a word in **C**. Look for synonyms and antonyms.

A	B	C
now sick more	and	tired quiet sound
touch peace safe	but	surely then go
slowly then	or	there less

   Try to put each pair into a sentence. Read the sentences aloud to the class.

4 **T 11.6** Listen to a conversation between two friends. What are they talking about? Write down all the word pairs you hear.

5 Look at the conversation on page 110. Practice it with your partner, paying particular attention to the stress and intonation.

READING AND SPEAKING
Have you ever wondered?

1 As you go through your day, do you ever wonder about things? Have you ever puzzled over these questions? Discuss them in groups. Which can you answer? Make notes of your ideas.

1. Why do we dream?
2. What are falling stars?
3. What would happen if the gravity on Earth was suddenly turned off?
4. Why do airplanes take longer to fly west than east?
5. What would happen if there was no dust?
6. What is the origin of the @ symbol?

2 Read the answers to the questions on pp. 94–95. Check your ideas and discuss them with your group.

Unit 11 • In your dreams 93

Have you ever wondered?
Answers to some important questions in life

1 Why do we dream?

Two different schools of thought exist as to why we dream: the physiological school and the psychological school. Both, however, agree that we dream during the REM, or rapid eye movement, phase of sleep. During this phase of sleep, our closed eyes dart rapidly around and our brain activity peaks.

The physiological theory centers upon how our brains function during the REM phase. Those who believe this theory say that we dream to exercise the brain cells. When awake, our brains constantly transmit and receive messages and keep our bodies in perpetual motion. Dreams replace this function.

Psychological theorists of dreams focus on our thoughts and emotions, and say that dreams deal with immediate concerns in our lives, such as unfinished business from the day. Dreams can, in fact, (1)___. Connections between dreams and the human psyche have been made for thousands of years. The Greek philosopher Aristotle wrote in his *Parva Naturalia*, over 2,200 years ago, of a connection between dreams and emotional needs. Sweet dreams!

2 What are falling stars?

Contrary to popular belief, "falling (or shooting) stars" are not stars at all, but meteors, solid bodies that travel through space. Meteors (2)___ to huge objects weighing many tons, which are visible to the naked eye at night. Most meteors, except the really huge ones, burn up when they enter the Earth's atmosphere. If they do land successfully, they are renamed meteorites.

Usually meteors travel together in swarms like bees. Nature's spectacular fireworks show, a "meteor shower," comes into view when these swarms hit the Earth's atmosphere and then fall towards the Earth in a brilliant display of light.

3 What would happen if the gravity on Earth was suddenly turned off?

Supposing we could magically turn off gravity. Would buildings and other structures float away? What happened would depend on how strongly the things were attached to the Earth. The Earth is rotating at quite a speed, (3)___. If you spin something around your head on a string it goes around in a circle until you let go of the string. Then it flies off in a straight line. "Switching off" gravity would be like letting go of the string. Things not attached to the Earth would fly off in a straight line. People in buildings would suddenly shoot upwards at a great speed until they hit the ceiling. Most things outside would fly off into space. Some things, like trees and many buildings, which are rooted into the Earth, would not find it so easy to fly off.

4 Why do airplanes take longer to fly west than east?

It can take five hours to go west to east from New York to London, but seven hours to travel east to west from London to New York. The reason for the difference is an atmospheric phenomenon (4)___. The jet stream is a very high altitude wind which always blows from the west to the east across the Atlantic. The planes moving at a constant air speed thus go faster from west to east, when they are moving with the wind, than in the opposite direction.

5 What would happen if there was no dust?

Most of us who have ever cleaned a house would be much happier if there was less dust. However, without dust there would be less rainfall and sunsets would be less beautiful. Rain is formed when water molecules in the air collect around particles of dust. When the collected water becomes heavy enough (5)___. Thus water vapor would be much less likely to turn to rain without the dust particles.

The water vapor and dust particles also reflect the rays of the sun. At sunrise and sunset, when the sun is below the horizon, the dust and water vapor molecules reflect the longer, red, rays of light in such a way that we can see them for more time. The more dust particles in the air, the more colorful the sunrise or sunset.

6 What is the origin of the @ symbol?

The most common theory that the little @ in e-mail addresses, commonly referred to as the "at sign," stemmed from the tired hands of medieval monks. During the Middle Ages, before the invention of printing presses, every letter of a word had to be painstakingly transcribed by hand in Latin for each copy of a book. The monks that performed these tedious copying duties looked for ways to reduce the number of individual strokes for common words. Although *ad*, a Latin word for *at*, is quite short, it was so common that the monks thought it would be quicker and easier to shorten it even more. As a result, they looped the "d" around the "a" and eliminated two strokes of the pen.

With the introduction of e-mail the popularity of the @ symbol grew. (6)___. For instance, *joe@uselessknowledge.com*. There is no one universal name for the sign, but countries have found different ways to describe it. Several languages use words that associate the shape with some type of animal. These include:

snabel—Danish for "elephant's trunk"
klammeraffe—German for "hanging monkey"
papaki—Greek for "little duck"
kukac—Hungarian for "worm"
dalphaengi—Korean for "snail"
grisehale—Norwegian for "pig's tail"
sobachka—Russian for "little dog"

Reading

3 Read the texts again. These lines have been removed from them. Which text does each come from?

   a. moving at over a thousand miles per hour at the equator.
   b. It separates a person's online user name from their mail server address.
   c. range in size from that of a pinhead
   d. the water droplets fall to the earth as rain
   e. teach us things about ourselves that we are unaware of
   f. known as the jet stream

4 Answer the questions.
   1. What does REM stand for?
   2. What kind of things do dreams deal with?
   3. What is the difference between a meteor and a meteorite?
   4. What travel like swarms of bees?
   5. What would happen to buildings and the people inside them if gravity was turned off?
   6. How does the jet stream affect how fast planes fly?
   7. What would happen to rain and sunsets if there was no dust?
   8. Why did the monks invent the @ sign?
   9. What is the @ sign called in different languages?

Vocabulary work

Find the highlighted words in the texts. Try to figure out their meaning from the contexts.

What do you think?

- Which questions did you find most interesting?
- Which facts were new to you? Which did you already know? Use some of these phrases to express your reactions.

I already knew that . . .	Did you know that . . . ?
What surprised me was . . .	Everyone knows that . . .
I don't believe that . . .	I had no idea that . . .

- What do *you* call the @ sign? Which language's animal words do you think best describe it?
- Small children often ask lots of "Why" questions.

  Why is the grass green?   Why doesn't our cat talk to me?

Think of some good "Why" questions about the world. In pairs, try to answer them as if you were talking to a child. (Kids will often answer with another "Why?" question!)

Why doesn't our cat talk to me?
Because cats can't talk.
Why can't cat's talk?
Because . . .

Unit 11 · In your dreams 95

LISTENING AND SPEAKING
The interpretation of dreams

1 Everybody dreams, but some people remember their dreams better than others. Discuss these questions in groups.
   1. Did you dream last night? Can you remember anything about it?
   2. What often happens when you wake up from a dream and try to describe it to someone?
   3. What do you think are common themes in dreams?

2 Read these descriptions of dreams. Discuss what you think each dream might mean.

1.
Fall guy
Many times, as I'm going to sleep, I dream that I am walking along the road and suddenly trip up and fall towards the pavement. I always wake up before I hit the ground. Why do I dream this?
J.H., SEATTLE, WASHINGTON

2.
Underneath it all
My dreams are often set in a small decaying cellar. I always wake up feeling bad about life when this happens. What does this dream mean?
D.J., WINNIPEG, CANADA

3.
Hidden treasure
I am digging in the garden of my childhood home and uncover a box of treasure. My life has been pretty bad lately. Does my dream indicate a change for the better?
P.T., SWINDON, UK

3 Read the interpretations of the dreams on page 111. Which do you think goes with each dream? Why? Compare them with your ideas.

4 **T 11.7** Listen to Paul describing a dream. What is really strange about the dream? Are these statements true or false? Correct the false ones.
   1. Paul describes himself as a sensible, rational person.
   2. The dream took place in his hometown.
   3. In the dream, he and his girlfriend had arranged to meet in front of the station.
   4. His girlfriend had a similar dream.
   5. His girlfriend had never visited his hometown.
   6. He believes their dreams were the result of a TV program they'd been watching.

Language work

Read the tapescript on page 139.
1. Find four things in the story that Paul describes as *strange*.
2. Find other words which are similar in meaning to *strange*.

What do you think?

- Discuss Paul's dream in your groups and try to interpret it. Share your ideas with the class.
- Describe any memorable dreams that you have had.
- Do you ever have the same dream or dreams with common features?

WRITING Narrative writing 2—Linking words and expressions **p. 124**

EVERYDAY ENGLISH
Moans and groans

It's not fair!
What a pain!
I don't believe it!

1 Read the complaints in **A**. Match them with a response in **B**. Which of the items in the box do they refer to?

> a leather jacket   e-mail   boots   ordering by phone
> a bookcase   a TV program   a package   ~~a test~~

A	B
1. [e] I could kick myself. As soon as I'd handed it in, I remembered what the answer was. *a test*	a. What a pain! Have you tried calling the computer helpline?
2. [ ] I can't believe it! I've spent all morning trying to send this, and *all I get* is "Ooops! Your message wasn't sent. Try again later."	b. Go easy on me! I was in a hurry. Anyway, they're not *that* muddy.
3. [ ] These instructions don't make any sense to me at all. If you can follow them, you're a genius.	c. I'm awfully sorry, sir. I'm afraid there's nothing I can do about it. It's out of my hands.
4. [ ] It's not fair. I'd been looking forward to watching it all day and then the phone goes and rings!	d. I know, it drives me crazy. But worse still is that you never get to speak to a real person anyway!
5. [ ] How many times do I have to tell you? Take them off *before* you come into the house!	e. Oh, I hate it when that happens! But do you think you still passed?
6. [ ] You've got to be kidding. You promised you'd deliver it by Thursday at the latest. Now you're saying next week!	f. It's such a shame. It would have gone so well with your white jeans.
7. [ ] I went away to think about it, and of course, when I went back it was gone. I wish I'd just bought it then and there.	g. Don't ask me! I had exactly the same trouble trying to put together a nightstand.
8. [ ] What a waste of time! Ten minutes listening to music and "All our lines are busy. Thank you for waiting."	h. Typical! And who was it? Anyone interesting?

2 **T 11.8** Listen and check your answers. Read them aloud with a partner and add another line.

> A I could kick myself. As soon as I'd handed it in, I remembered what the answer was.
> B Oh, I hate it when that happens! But do you think you still passed?
> A Who knows? I'll just have to wait and see.

Music *of* English 🎵

When people moan about something, there is an exaggeration on the rise and fall of the word with the main stress.

I don't believe it!   *It's not fair!*

T 11.9 Listen and repeat.

3 What are some of the events in a typical day in your life? For each event think of something to moan about.

What a pain! I got up and had to wait forever before the shower was free. But worse still, the water was freezing cold!

4 Do you have any moans and groans about anything that's happened recently in your country or in the world?

"Press 1 for classical, press 2 for easy listening, press 3 for jazz."

Unit 11 · In your dreams   97

12 It's never too late

Articles • Determiners • Hot words—*life, time* • Linking and commenting

TEST YOUR GRAMMAR

1 Tell the story of Mary's grandfather, matching a line from **A** with a line from **C**. Use the correct article from **B** to connect the lines. Tell the story to a partner.

My grandfather used to be a judge. He retired ...

2 **T 12.1** Listen and check. What extra information do you hear?

A	B	C
1. My grandfather used to be		dinner with him.
2. He retired		captain of the ship.
3. He decided to go on		ocean cruise.
4. He enjoyed	a/an	cruise very much.
5. He sailed all around	one	year before last.
6. He met	the	judge.
7. He invited her to have	no article	love at any age.
8. They got along really well with		another.
9. My grandfather says you can find		world.
10. They were married by		attractive widow.

THE PACE OF LIFE
Articles and determiners

1 Take the quiz about your pace of life. Discuss your answers with a partner. Turn to page 111 and find out what kind of person you are. Do you agree?

2 Find these highlighted words in the quiz. Underline the nouns that follow. Which are followed by *of*?

enough	the whole	all	each	plenty
a great deal	hardly any	several		none
no	(a) few	(a) little	most	

3 These lines are similar to those in the quiz, but not the same. Find them in the quiz. What are the differences?

1. I leave sufficient time for relaxation.
2. Nonstop all of the time.
3. More than enough things.
4. Lots of enthusiasm.
5. Very few, just a couple of minor things.
6. There aren't any uncompleted projects.
7. I see every one of my projects through to the end.
8. I don't have any patience.
9. I have hardly any hobbies or leisure time.
10. In quite a few ways.
11. In all kinds of ways.
12. Nearly all of the time by e-mail.

How well do you

1 How would you describe the pace of your life?
 a. Easygoing. I just take life as it comes.
 b. Pretty fast, but I leave enough time for relaxation.
 c. At times frantic, at times relaxed.
 d. Nonstop the whole time, but I like it that way.

2 How do you tackle all the things you have to do each day?
 a. I do the things I feel like doing, but there aren't many of those.
 b. I prioritize. I do the important things and put off all the other stuff.
 c. There's either not enough time to do every little thing or too much time with nothing to do. I find this difficult.
 d. I have a daily "to do" list that I check off after each item is completed.

3 How many things have you begun and not finished in the last few years?
 a. Plenty of things. I begin with a great deal of enthusiasm but then get bored.
 b. Hardly any, just one or two minor things.
 c. Several things. Sometimes I get distracted and move from one thing to another.
 d. None. There are no uncompleted projects in my life. I see each of my projects through to the end before I start the next.

98 Unit 12 • It's never too late

4 **When do you switch off your cell phone?**
   a. Do most people have cell phones these days? I haven't gotten round to getting one yet.
   b. In some public places and when I need some peace and quiet.
   c. Not as often as I should.
   d. Only if I have to.

5 **How punctual are you?**
   a. I don't waste time worrying about it.
   b. Being late is impolite and inefficient, so I try to be punctual.
   c. I like to be on time in theory, but in practice I'm often late.
   d. I'm always on time. I have no patience with people who are late.

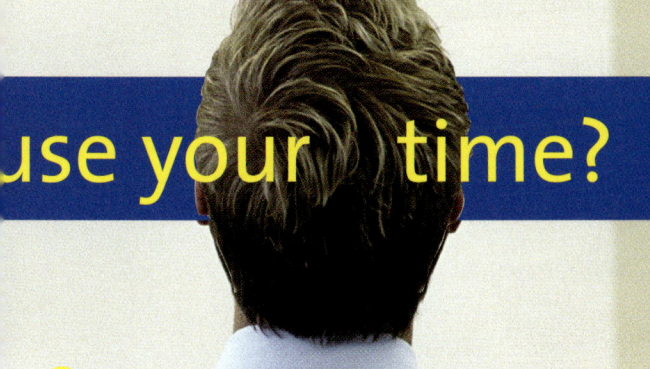

6 **How do you spend your leisure time?**
   a. Doing a little of this and a little of that. I don't know where my time goes.
   b. I recharge my batteries with a few hobbies and by being with friends.
   c. I keep trying different things that people suggest, but nothing really grabs me.
   d. I have few hobbies and little leisure time. I try to put all of my time to good use.

7 **How do you keep in touch with friends?**
   a. I wait for them to get in touch with me.
   b. In several ways—e-mails, text messages—but I also like to call them for a nice chat.
   c. In any way I can—but it can be difficult. I think, "I must contact X," but time passes and I realize I haven't.
   d. Most of the time by e-mail. It's quick and efficient.

8 **Which of these is closest to your philosophy on life?**
   a. Whatever will be will be.
   b. Life is not a dress rehearsal.
   c. There is a season for everything.
   d. Seize the day.

4 What is the difference between these pairs of sentences?

   I have a few hobbies.   I have a little leisure time.
   I have few hobbies.   I have little leisure time.

5 Is there a difference in meaning between these sentences?

   I completed **each** project.   I completed **every** project.

   Which can mean you had only two projects? Which *can't* mean you had only two projects? Which can mean you had lots of projects?

GRAMMAR SPOT

Determiners
Determiners help identify nouns and express quantity.

1 Look at the examples. Which determiners go with which nouns? Which group expresses quantity?

the other another many other his only such a what a	book books good book	both neither each/every little all the whole no	book books time

2 Determiners can join a noun using *of + the/my/our/this/that*, etc. What expressions can you make from these examples?

both neither each all some none	of	the my those	book books time

▶▶ Grammar Reference 12.1 p. 154

PRACTICE

Talking about you

1 Complete the sentences with determiners which make them true for you.
   1. I have _____ time to relax.
   2. _____ my friends think I work too hard.
   3. _____ my teachers think I work hard.
   4. I spent _____ weekend relaxing.
   5. I have _____ interests and hobbies.
   6. _____ my hobbies are sports.
   7. _____ my parents look like me.
   8. _____ my relatives have fair hair.
   9. My aunt gives _____ us birthday presents.
   10. My grandparents watch TV _____ time.

Discussing grammar

2 Work with a partner. What is the difference in meaning between these pairs of sentences?

1. I spoke to all the students in the class.
   I spoke to each student in the class.
2. None of them knew the answer.
   Neither of them knew the answer.
3. The doctor's here.
   A doctor's here.
4. There's a man at the door.
   There's some man at the door.
5. There's a pair of socks missing.
   There's a couple of socks missing.
6. Whole families were evacuated from their homes.
   All the families were evacuated from their homes.

3 Match a line in **A** with a line in **B**.

A	B
Would you like Do all birds lay Where did I put	eggs? the egg? an egg?

A	B
I have two cars. Borrow It was great to see I have five nieces. I gave $10 to	each one. everyone. either one.

A	B
Love A love The love	I have for you is forever. is everything. of animals is vital for a vet.
Both All Every	my friends like dancing. person in my class is friendly. my parents are Canadian.

4 **T 12.2** Listen and respond to the lines with a sentence from Exercise 3.

Do any of your friends like dancing?

What do you mean, "any"? All my friends like dancing!

T 12.3 Listen and check. Pay particular attention to stress and intonation. Look at the tapescript on page 140 and practice the conversations with a partner.

SPOKEN ENGLISH Using demonstratives and determiners

Demonstratives and determiners are often found in idiomatic language.
Look at these examples of the demonstratives *this*, *that*, *these*, and *those* from the quiz on page 98.

> (I like) doing a little of *this* and a little of *that*.
> Most people have cell phones *these days*.
> … but there aren't many of *those*.

Find examples of the determiners *each*, *every*, and *all* in the quiz.

5 Demonstratives—*this/that/these/those*

Complete the sentences with the correct demonstrative.

1. What's _____ song you're singing?
2. Look at _____ ladybug on my hand!
3. Did you hear _____ storm in the middle of the night?
4. Mmm! _____ strawberries are delicious!
5. Take _____ dirty shoes off! I've just cleaned in here.
6. I can't stand _____ weather. It's really getting me down.
7. Who was _____ man you were talking to _____ morning?
8. Do you remember when we were young? _____ were the days!
9. Children have no respect for authority _____ days, do they?

T 12.4 Listen and check.

6 Determiners—*each*, *every*, or *all*

T 12.5 Listen to some short conversations. What is each about? Complete the replies. They all contain expressions with *each*, *every*, or *all*. Practice the conversations with a partner.

1. **A** What was the meal like?
   B …
2. **A** Did you apologize to all the guests?
   B …
3. **A** They didn't all pass, did they?
   B …
4. **A** Sorry, I only have 50 cents on me.
   B …
5. **A** When do you think you'll get there?
   B …
6. **A** Want to grab a bite to eat?
   B …

WRITING Adding emphasis in writing—People of influence *p. 125*

LISTENING AND SPEAKING
Happy days

1 Work in small groups. What is the average life expectancy in your country? Suggest ages for these stages of life. What is typical behavior for each stage? Give examples and discuss with the whole class.

```
0 - [ ]   infancy
[ ] - [ ] childhood
[ ] - [ ] teenage years
[ ] - [ ] young adulthood
[ ] - [ ] middle age
[ ] - [ ] old age
```

2 You are going to listen to Bernie, Hayley, Tony, and Tommy talking about themselves. Here are some of the things they said (two for each person). Which stage of life do you think they are at?

1. I want to see the world, meet lots of people, get a good career before I settle down.
2. This time though, after the operation I knew right away it would be OK.
3. We have buckets and spades.
4. Lizzie and I are content just to putter in the vegetable patch, or cut the grass, or weed the flower beds.
5. Most of us just get off on dancing.
6. I think the world has gone to pot.
7. It's got big, big wheels, hugest wheels ever.
8. These days the only thing that makes me unhappy is meeting people who don't realize what a gift life is.

3 **T 12.6** Listen to the four people. After each one discuss these questions.

1. At which stage of life is the person?
2. Which lines in Exercise 2 did he or she say?
3. What does the person do or say that is typical or not typical for their age?
4. What makes the person happy or unhappy?

What do you think?

- Which stage of life do you think is the best or worst? Why?
- Are there advantages and disadvantages for each stage? Discuss.
- Do you know people who you think are typical or not typical for their age? Are you?

READING AND SPEAKING
You're never too old

1 What age do you consider to be old? Think of some "old" people you know.

> How old are they?
> What are they like?
> What do they do every day?
> Which of these are typical for old people?
> - having trouble sleeping
> - liking routine
> - going to college
> - studying foreign languages
> - going to church
> - talking about the past
> - losing your memory
> - using the Internet
> - living in the center of a city
> - watching TV

2 Read the text quickly. Which of the activities in Exercise 1 are part of Mary Hobson's life? Explain the title, "A Life in the Day."

3 Read the text again. Find the **highlighted** lines and answer the questions about them.

1. l.04 What is "it"? Why does "it" do this?
2. l.10 What is "it"? How did Marcus Aurelius help Mary?
3. l.22 What does she work at for nothing? What does this imply about Mary's lifestyle?
4. l.24 Who is "he"? Who is "some old bat"?
5. l.30 What was hell for who? What did Mary do about it?
6. l.35 What was the session? What did Mary do in it?
7. l.47 Is "the time of your life" a good or bad time? What was the time of Mary's life?
8. l.55 Why do they think this?
9. l.65 What is "it"? What does Mary mean by this?
10. l.67 What is "it"? Why does she sleep so badly?

A life in the day

Mary Hobson, 77, gained a degree in Russian in her sixties and a PhD at 74. A mother of four, she lives in south London.

I've started to learn ancient Greek. It doesn't urge you to communicate, only to learn, and I find the early hours of the morning the perfect time for that. I love ritual and routine. I wait until 6 A.M. to have tea; at 7 A.M. I phone my youngest daughter and we start the day with a chat. At 7:30 I make breakfast—All-Bran, wholemeal toast, and a pot of black coffee—and I take it back to bed along with the Roman emperor Marcus Aurelius.

I am a dedicated atheist. I regard religion as complete lunacy. You've got only one opportunity to be alive: for goodness' sake don't waste it waiting for an afterlife. I read Marcus Aurelius every day; it was his philosophy that got me through my son Matthew's death, four years ago in a motorcycle accident. Aurelius said: "What we cannot bear removes us from life." Matthew's death was such a waste. At first I would rather have been dead too, but then I thought: "No. I mustn't do less. I must do more!"

After a bath I spend the morning translating. A special committee was convened to organize the translation of the works of Pushkin for his centenary. Unpaid, of course. I'm an expert at working for nothing. Poor old Pushkin: some of his letters were scandalous. Really very rude indeed. How was he to know that, 200 years later, some old bat would be poring over every line?

I am what you might call a late developer. I was 40 before I wrote my first novel, 62 when I went to university. My husband, Neil, was a talented jazz musician, but at 25 he developed a cerebral abscess, losing his speech and the use of the right side of his body. It was hell for him and a nightmare for us. We were so broke, we lived on government assistance for ages. When things got really bad, I'd collect up old china and give it to the children to smash out their frustrations on the wall outside.

I wrote my first novel while Neil had his weekly music therapy. That 50-minute session was all I had. I used to sit in the ABC cafe in Earls Court and write and write while couples had life-and-death quarrels around me. Neil was terribly difficult. None of it was his fault, of course, but after 28 years I thought: "It's not my fault either." I was going down with him. I left and Matthew stayed with him to stop me going back—I was very grateful for that.

Having snatched a bit of life back, I had to do something with it. My daughter Emma gave me *War and Peace*, and I loved it so much. Then it hit me: I hadn't read it at all, I'd only read a translation, and I so longed to read the actual words. A marvelous elderly Russian lady taught me the basics and I enrolled in the Russian-

Mary Hobson

by Caroline Scott

WINNER OF THE PUSHKIN GOLD MEDAL FOR TRANSLATION

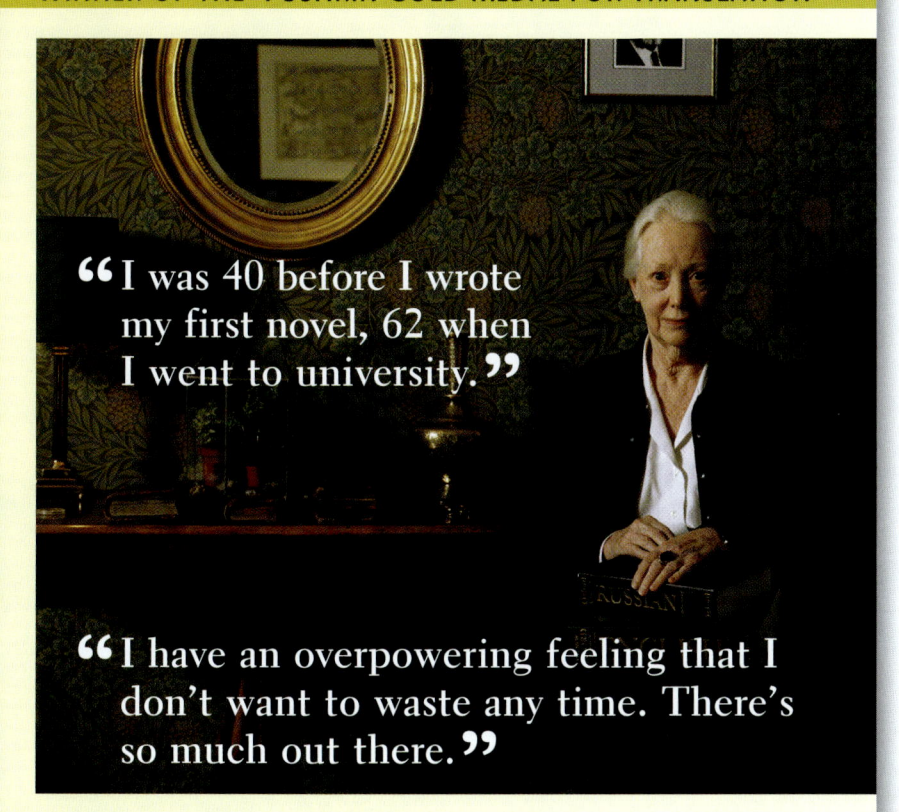

> "I was 40 before I wrote my first novel, 62 when I went to university."

> "I have an overpowering feeling that I don't want to waste any time. There's so much out there."

language degree course at the University of London. People talk about "the time of their lives." Well, that was mine. Don't let anyone tell you your memory goes with age. It's there if you want it enough. Gradually I forced it into action—it was such an exhilarating experience. Oh, the joy of learning!

I have such good friends. After a late lunch, I might go and play Scrabble with a Russian lady. I write poetry en route, on buses and trains. I love London. Give me the town over the country any day. I try to go to Moscow every year in the coldest weather. My Russian friends think I'm mad; it hits minus 40 and they find it hellish. I adore lying in bed listening to snow being scraped from the pavements.

I have an overpowering feeling that I don't want to waste any time. There's so much out there. I won't be able to get about forever, so when I can't stagger down my front steps, I'll perfect my Greek. I order my groceries on the Internet, so I have everything sent. As long as I have my books I'll be happy.

If I'm not going out, I make supper and get into bed, simply because my feet are awful. Then I phone everyone I can think of. I can't bear TV—it makes me feel as if everyone else is living and I'm only watching. I don't have a newspaper; I get my news through the radio. I sleep rottenly, so I have it on all night. Dreams are horrendous. Mine are all about anxiety and loss. I much prefer the day—at least you know you're in charge.

Language work

There is *one* mistake in each of these sentences. Find it and discuss why it is wrong with a partner. Check your answers in the text.

1. I make breakfast and I take it back to the bed.
2. I am a dedicated atheist. My husband was talented jazz musician.
3. You've got only an opportunity to be alive.
4. I enrolled in the Russian-language degree course at University of London.
5. I try to go to Moscow every year in coldest weather.
6. Having snatched a bit of the life back, I had to do something with it.
7. Give me the town over a country.
8. I make supper and get into bed, simply because the feet are awful.

What do you think?

- It's easy to think of all the advantages of being young and the disadvantages of being old. But try it the other way around. Work in two groups.

    Group A List all the disadvantages of being young.

    Group B List all the advantages of being old.

- Find a partner from the other group and discuss your lists.
- Discuss as a class. What do you think is the best age to be in life?

VOCABULARY AND LISTENING
Hot words—*life* and *time*

1 Work with a partner. Complete the expressions below with either the word *life* or *time*. Use a dictionary to help.

Having the time of your life!

not on your _____	you can bet your _____
take your _____	better luck next _____
get a _____	get a new lease on _____
kill _____	third _____'s the charm
it's high _____	for the _____ being
no _____ to lose	stand the test of _____
that's _____	live _____
on _____	in the nick of _____
any old _____	right on _____
a cushy _____	make good _____

2 Complete these lines with an expression from Exercise 1.
1. No need to hurry. Take …
2. For goodness' sake hurry up. There's no …
3. The operation was so successful that Grandpa got a new …
4. Shakespeare's writing is still relevant today. It's really stood …
5. I got to the bank in the … It was just about to close.
6. You can give them back any … I'm not going skiing again until next year.

3 **T 12.7** Listen to the conversations. What are the people talking about? Which of the expressions from Exercise 1 do you hear? Turn to page 141 and practice the conversations with your partner.

A song

4 **T 12.8** Close your books and listen to a song called "That's Life," recorded by Frank Sinatra and the British singer Robbie Williams. Then read the words on this page. There are many differences. Listen again and note them all.

5 **T 12.8** Listen again and sing along!

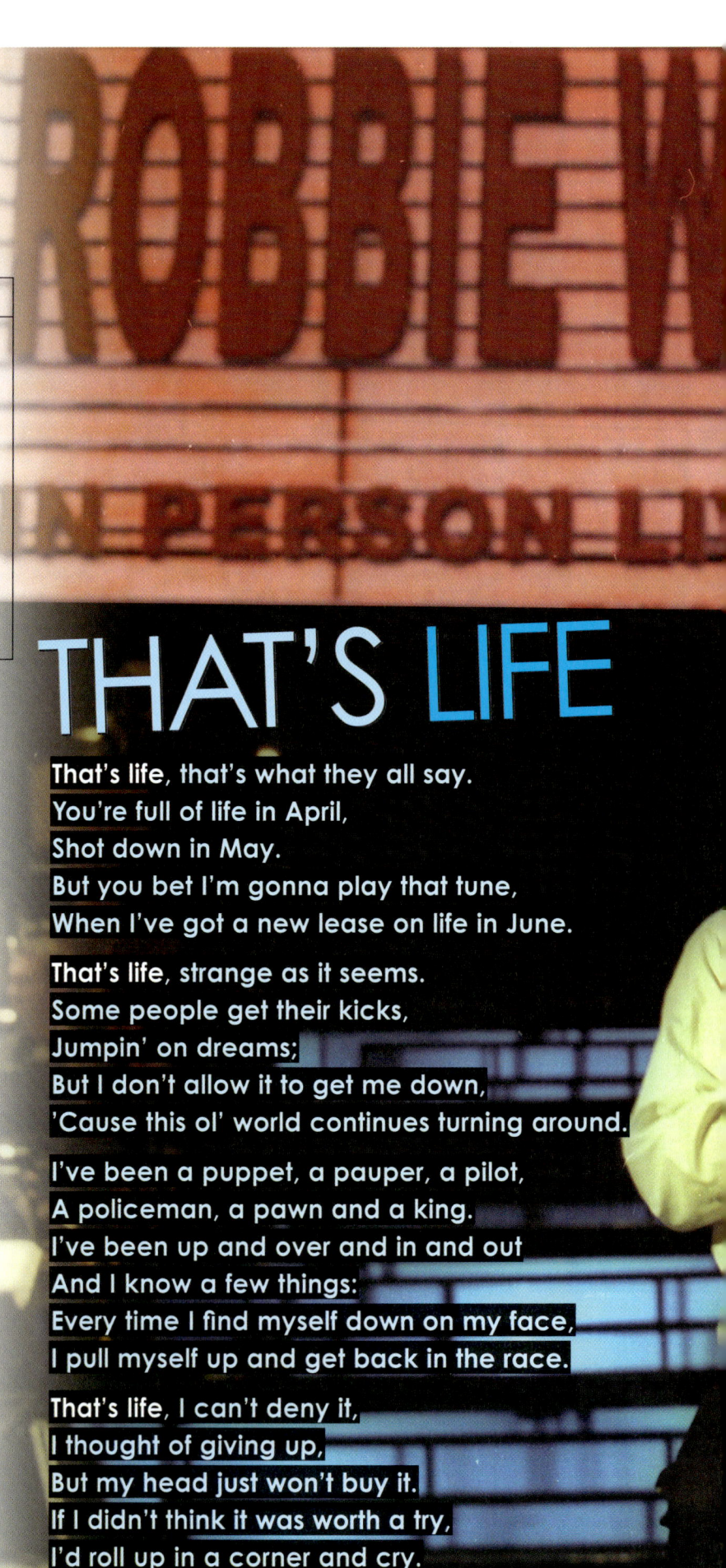

THAT'S LIFE

That's life, that's what they all say.
You're full of life in April,
Shot down in May.
But you bet I'm gonna play that tune,
When I've got a new lease on life in June.

That's life, strange as it seems.
Some people get their kicks,
Jumpin' on dreams;
But I don't allow it to get me down,
'Cause this ol' world continues turning around.

I've been a puppet, a pauper, a pilot,
A policeman, a pawn and a king.
I've been up and over and in and out
And I know a few things:
Every time I find myself down on my face,
I pull myself up and get back in the race.

That's life, I can't deny it,
I thought of giving up,
But my head just won't buy it.
If I didn't think it was worth a try,
I'd roll up in a corner and cry.

EVERYDAY ENGLISH
Linking and commenting

1 Look at these lines from tapescript 12.6. The expressions in **bold** link or comment on what has been said or what is going to be said. They are mainly adverbs.

> **Personally**, I'm just happy to be alive.
> **You see**, I'd recently gotten married ...
> **Anyway**, I had some tests ...
> **In fact**, my body rejected ...

Find other examples from the tapescripts on pages 140–141.

2 Read these conversations. Choose the correct linking or commenting expression.

1. A Did you see the game last night?
   B No, but *apparently / obviously* it was a good one. We won, didn't we?
   A *Probably / Actually*, it was a tie, but it was really exciting.

2. A What do you think of Claire's new boyfriend?
   B *Personally / Certainly*, I can't stand him. I think he'll dump her like all the rest. *Ideally / However*, that's her problem, not mine.
   A Poor old Claire! She always picks the wrong ones, doesn't she? *Anyway / Honestly*, we'll find out soon enough.

3. A I don't know how you can afford to buy all those fabulous clothes!
   B *Still / Hopefully*, I'm going to get a bonus this month. My boss promised. *After all / Presumably*, I did earn the company over $100,000 last year. *Basically / Absolutely*, I deserve it.

4. A She said some terrible things to me. I hate her!
   B *Generally speaking / All the same*, I think you should apologize to her. *If you ask me / Apparently*, you lose your temper too easily. You're being very childish. It's time you both grew up!
   A What? I never thought I'd hear you speak to me like that.
   B *Still / Honestly*, I'm not taking sides. I just think you should make up.

5. A So, Billy. You say that this is the last record you're ever going to make?
   B *Surely / Definitely*.
   A But *surely / actually* you realize how upset your fans are going to be?
   B *Obviously / Hopefully*, I don't want to hurt anyone, but *certainly / basically*, I'm fed up with pop music. I'd like to do something else. *After all / Ideally*, I'd like to get into movies.

T 12.9 Listen and check your answers. Practice some of the conversations.

3 Complete these with a suitable line.

1. They had a dreadful vacation. **Apparently, ...**
2. It should have been a happy marriage. **After all, ...**
3. I know you don't want to go to Harry's party. **All the same, ...**
4. I had the interview yesterday. **Hopefully, ...**
5. I'd rather you didn't let this go any further. **Obviously, ...**
6. I couldn't believe it, he just walked out and left her. **Presumably, ...**
7. I don't like flying very much. **As a matter of fact, ...**
8. So that's that. All's well that ends well. **Anyway, ...**

Getting Information

▶ **UNIT 10** p. 83

ÖTZI THE ICEMAN

He died 5,300 years ago. He was 46 years old and 5 feet 2 inches tall. He had a beard.

His last meal was goat steak and bread baked in charcoal.

He wore goatskin leggings, a deerskin jacket, a thick grass cape, and a bearskin hat.

He stuffed his leather shoes with grass to keep out the cold.

He lived his entire life in a world just 50 kilometers across.

He knew how to look after himself. He had over 70 items in his possession, including flints for skinning animals and sharpening tools. In his backpack he carried herbs with pharmaceutical properties, dried fruit, and flint and tinder for starting fires.

He was probably a herdsman or hunter, but on this day he was a warrior. He had an axe and a longbow, and arrows tipped with a flint. No one knows how the battle started. Perhaps Ötzi and his companions deliberately entered enemy territory, or perhaps they were ambushed, or attacked one another.

From the DNA on his clothing and weapons, and the injuries to his body, Ötzi's last and fatal fight can be reconstructed with some precision.

Ötzi stabbed one of his enemies with his flint dagger. He shot an arrow into another and managed to retrieve the valuable weapon before shooting it again. He killed or wounded at least three men, but the hand-to-hand fighting was ferocious. Ötzi tried to hold off one assailant and suffered a deep wound in one hand that left three fingers useless.

Ötzi put up a fierce fight until an arrow, fired from behind, entered his shoulder and penetrated close to his lung. Ötzi retreated into the mountains, but not before lifting a wounded companion onto his back. The blood of the injured man mixed with Ötzi's, soaking into his jacket.

Finally, high in the Ötzal Alps, Ötzi staggered into a small ravine and collapsed. It took two more days before he died, and the ice closed over him.

▶ **UNIT 11** p. 93

VOCABULARY AND PRONUNCIATION
Word pairs

T 11.6

A Are you going to take a vacation this year?

B I'd love to—but we'll have to wait and see. We're kind of broke at the moment.

A We're hoping to rent that farmhouse in Vermont, but it's touch and go whether we will.

B Why's that?

A Well, I don't know if I can get the time off work.

B But I thought they were good about giving you time off.

A Yeah, they are, by and large, but we're a small company and we have to cover for each other, so there's a lot of give and take.

B Yeah, I can see that. At least *you* got away last year. I'm sick and tired of not being able to go anywhere.

A You get away now and then, don't you?

B More "then" than "now." We used to spend the occasional weekend in the country, but since the kids came along it's more difficult. Oh, for the peace and quiet of the countryside—uh, but I don't suppose we'd get much peace or quiet, even if we *could* afford to go, what with three kids and two dogs.

A Is Chris fed up too?

B You know Chris. Never complains, just grins and bears it.

A I tell you what. If we do manage to get that farmhouse, why don't you all join us? It's huge.

B Oh, that's so kind! Uh, but I don't know. Wouldn't we be spoiling your vacation? What would Pat think? What if …

A Oh, just come along! The offer's there—you can take it or leave it!

B I can't tell you how much I appreciate it. It would be great, but can I talk to Chris about it first?

A Of course. I'm sure you'll want to go through all the pros and cons together.

B I can't think of many cons. It's just too good to be true. Thank you so much.

A Well, as I said, the offer's there. Let's hope I get the time off work—we'll have a great time together.

UNIT 11 p. 96

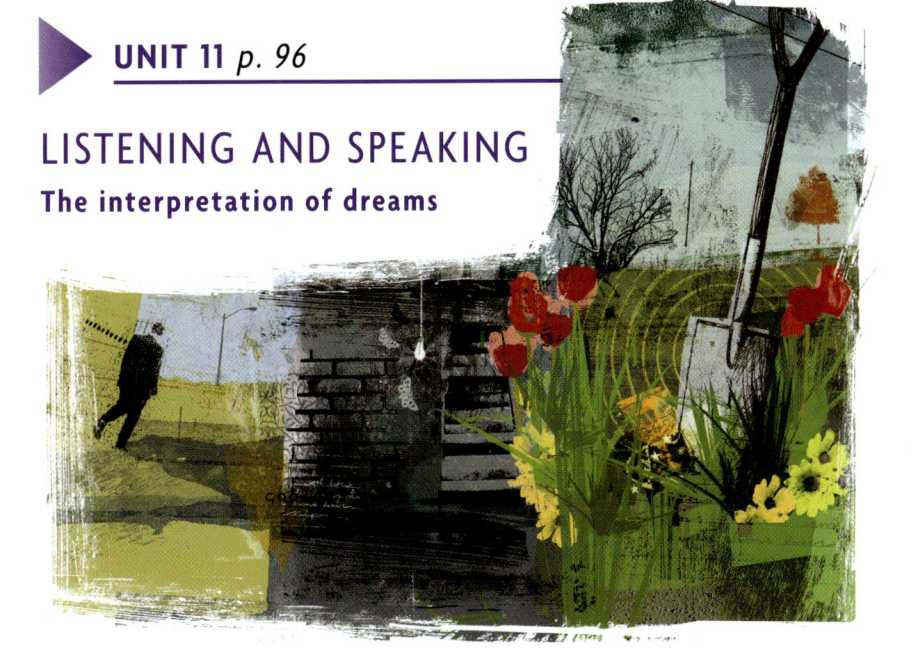

LISTENING AND SPEAKING
The interpretation of dreams

a. Buildings and houses are symbols of yourself. The upstairs represents your conscious mind and the lower floors and cellar your hidden self. The cramped feeling of the cellar indicates frustration and a need to expand your activities or thinking. Decayed or crumbling buildings indicate that your self-image has suffered. Treat yourself to a few activities that make you feel good about yourself.

b. This dream symbolizes rediscovering a part of yourself. There may be something that you have neglected or repressed. It could be that you had an ambition in life and only now have found the opportunity to try again.

The dream may also have a literal interpretation. If you're worried about finances, now may be the time to start a new venture.

c. This dream highlights a loss of self-control. It may represent your insecurity, a lack of self-confidence, a fear of failure, or an inability to cope with a situation. There could also be a literal interpretation. You may have noticed something unsafe—a loose stair rail, wobbly ladder, or insecure window. Check it out. The dream may be a warning.

UNIT 12 p. 98

THE PACE OF LIFE
How well do you use your time?

Answers to quiz

Mostly a answers
You're a daydreamer. Did you actually manage to finish the quiz? You have little control over your life. Chaos surrounds you. Perhaps you tell yourself that you are being creative, but the truth is you are frightened of failure so you don't try. Your abilities remain untested and your dreams unfulfilled.

Mostly b answers
You represent balance and common sense. Your ability to manage your life is impressive, and you know when to relax. You understand that the best decisions are never made in an atmosphere of pressure. You are able to meet deadlines and look ahead to make sure crises don't happen.

Mostly c answers
You live in hope that something or somebody will make everything in life work out for you. "I'll get around to it," you tell yourself. What you don't tell yourself is that you alone can manage your life. You are expert at putting things off till later and finding excuses when you do so. Forget these excuses. The right time is now.

Mostly d answers
You are certainly an achiever. Superman or superwoman. You know how to get a job done and you are proud of the way you manage your life. You are obsessive about putting every second of the day to the best use, and get irritated by people who are not like you and prefer to take life at a slower pace. Learn to relax a little. Remember, stress kills.

Writing

UNIT 7 ARGUING YOUR CASE—For and against

1. Do you send e-mails? If so, who to and when? What e-mails have you received or sent recently? Discuss with a partner, then with the class.

2. Is e-mail a good or a bad thing? Brainstorm ideas as a class. Divide the blackboard into two. Appoint two students to take notes, one for each column.

PROS (+)	CONS (–)

   Discuss your results. On balance, which side wins? What's your opinion?

3. Read through the article quickly. How many of the points you made are mentioned? How many other points did you make?

4. Study the article more carefully.
   1. How is the topic introduced?
   2. What personal examples does the writer include throughout the article?
   3. For each point on the plus side, underline the words and expressions used to connect the ideas.
      First of all, e-mail is easy.
   4. Compare the words and expressions used to connect the ideas on the minus side. Which are similar?
   5. How is the article concluded? How does the writer express his opinion?

5. Brainstorm the arguments for and against one of the topics below. Then write an introduction, the pros, the cons, and your conclusion (about 250 words).
   - The cell phone
   - Traveling the world in your 20s
   - Adult children living at home

Subject: E-mail—a good thing or a bad thing?

In recent years e-mail has become an increasingly important means of communication. However, in my opinion, like most things it has both advantages and disadvantages.

On the plus side:

- First of all, e-mail is easy. All you need is the appropriate software on your computer. There are no stamps to stick and no trips in the freezing cold to mailboxes.

- A second point is that e-mail is fast. No matter where you're sending your message, whether it's to the next street or to the other side of the planet, it takes only seconds to reach its destination. Nowadays, whenever I send regular mail (or "snail mail," as e-mail users call it), I can't believe that it's actually going to take days to reach its destination. How primitive!

- E-mail is not only fast, it is also cheap. Unlike long distance telephone calls, you pay no more for messages sent from the US to London, Ohio, or London, Ontario, or London, England.

- Also, e-mail messages are easily stored. Because they're electronic, saving an e-mail message you've received (and calling it back up again later) is a breeze.

- In addition to this, e-mail is environmentally friendly because, being electronic, it saves natural resources such as paper.

- Last but not least, e-mail is practically universal. Even my great aunt in rural Canada is using it these days.

On the minus side:

- Firstly, e-mail is impersonal. Unlike when face to face or in telephone conversations, it's difficult to get across subtle meanings in e-mail prose with no visual or voice clues.

- Secondly, it can be argued that e-mail is in fact too easy. You can write a message in a few seconds and send it off with one click. And once it's sent, you can't get back a message that may have been written in a fit of irritation or anger.

- Another point is that e-mail security is lax. As your e-mail message makes its way to its destination, it has to pass through other, public, systems. Anyone with the right technical know-how can intercept it without you knowing.

- Although, as stated above, it is an advantage that e-mail messages are easily stored, this can also be a disadvantage. If you say nasty things about your boss in a message, a saved copy can come back to haunt you in the future.

- A final and very important point is that e-mail can take over your life. Because it is so easy, you start getting more and more correspondence, and you end up spending most of your day reading and responding to floods of messages.

Overall, however, to my mind the pros of e-mail easily outweigh the cons, and e-mail is a good thing. It has transformed the world of communication in largely beneficial ways, and alongside text messaging, is now a major way of keeping in touch.

UNIT 8 DESCRIBING PLACES—My favorite part of town

1 What's your favorite town or city? Why do you like it? Which parts of it do you particularly like? Work with a partner and tell them about it.

2 Do the words in the box describe something positive, negative, or neutral?

Do they refer to a person, a place, or food? Or more than one?

> lively   dash around (v)   shabby   dull
> brand-new   snoring   a down-and-out
> cosmopolitan   pedestrian   buzz (v)
> trendy   boutiques   packed   flock (v)
> mouth-watering aromas   a magnet

3 Read the description of Soho. Which parts of Soho do the pictures show?

4 Work with your partner and decide where you could divide the text into paragraphs. What is the purpose of each paragraph? Think of a heading for each one and compare them with others in the class.

5 The description is part fact and part opinion. Find examples of both.

6 Underline examples of relative clauses and participles.

7 Write a description of your favorite part of town (about 250 words). Use the paragraph plan to help you.
   Paragraph 1: General / personal impressions
   Paragraph 2: Its history
   Paragraph 3: Its character
   Paragraph 4: Conclusion and/or final anecdote

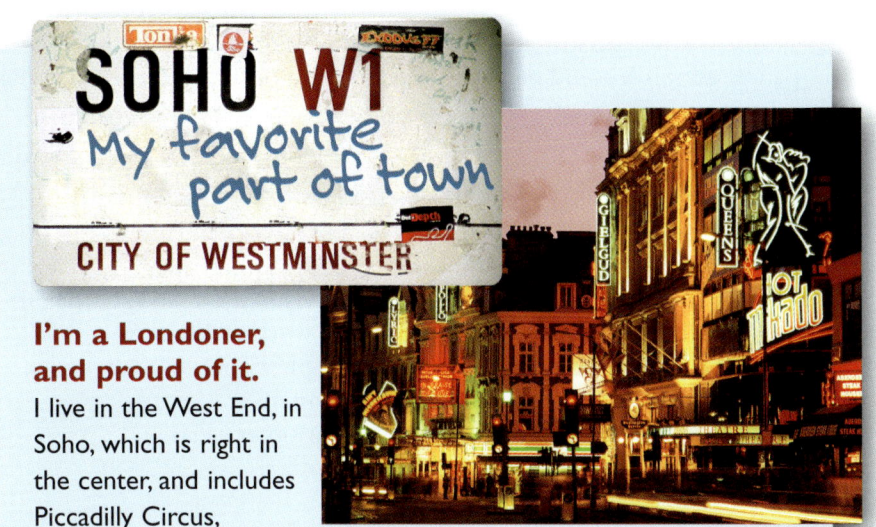

I'm a Londoner, and proud of it.

I live in the West End, in Soho, which is right in the center, and includes Piccadilly Circus, Shaftesbury Avenue, and Leicester Square. It's my favorite part of town. So why do I like it so much? It is always lively and colorful, with people dashing around, going about their business, which is mainly honest but not always. Some of the streets may be a bit shabby but life in Soho is never dull. There's a surprise round every corner—maybe a brand-new nightclub that wasn't there last week, a snoring down-and-out sleeping in a doorway, or a celebrity being pursued by paparazzi and fans. A sense of history pervades Soho. The name is derived from a hunting call, "So-ho," that hunters were heard to cry as they chased deer in what were the royal parklands. It has been a cosmopolitan area since the first immigrants, who were French Huguenots, arrived in the 1680s. They were followed by Germans, Russians, Poles, Greeks, and Italians. More recently there have been a lot of Chinese immigrants from Hong Kong. Gerrard Street, which is for pedestrians only, is the center of London's Chinatown, and buzzes all year round, but especially at the New Year celebrations in February. Many famous people have lived in Soho, including Mozart, Karl Marx, and the poet T.S. Eliot. It has a reputation for attracting artists, writers, poets, musicians, and people in the media. Shaftesbury Avenue is in the heart of London's theater distict, and there are endless clubs, pubs, trendy boutiques, and of course, restaurants. A large part of the Soho experience is to do with food. Soho is packed with European food shops and restaurants. Mouth-watering aromas are everywhere, from first thing in the morning till late at night. Soho is a genuine 24/7 part of town. Piccadilly Circus is like a magnet for young people. They flock from every corner of the world to sit on the steps under the statue of Eros, celebrating the freedom and friendship of youth. My mother, who grew up in London, used to say that if you wait long enough at Piccadilly Circus, you'll meet everyone you've ever known!

UNIT 9 WRITING FOR TALKING—What I want to talk about is ...

1. Think of *any* aspect of your life that you would like to tell other people about. It could be your job, a hobby, a person, a place, a special occasion, a news event. Write some notes about it. Ask and answer questions about it with a partner.

2. **T 9.13** Read and listen to someone talking about a man named Christopher and answer the questions.
   1. What is the speaker's relationship to Christopher?
   2. Why is he called "Cheap Christopher"? What does "stingy" mean?
   3. What do you learn about Christopher's work and family?
   4. Name some of the stingy things Christopher does.
   5. What's the stingiest thing he has ever done?
   6. What did he use to give his mother on Mother's Day?
   7. What is the speaker's opinion of Christopher?
   8. What does his wife say?

3. Now read the talk carefully and answer the questions.
   1. Underline the phrases that introduce each paragraph. Why are these words used?
   2. Underline *all* the questions in the text. These are *rhetorical questions*. What does this mean? Why are they used?
   3. Find examples of the speaker giving her personal opinion.
   4. Practice reading aloud the first paragraph with a partner.

Preparing your talk

4. Think of a title for the notes you made about your topic. Write a talk using these guidelines. Try to include some rhetorical questions.
   1. Give the title:
      The title of my talk is …
   2. Introduce your topic:
      I want to talk about X because …
      Today I'll be talking about X because …
   3. Give some background:
      Let's start with some background. …
      I've always been interested in …
      As you all probably know, …
   4. Hit your first point:
      First, …
      What happened was this, …
   5. Move to new points:
      I'd now like to turn to …
      Moving on, …
      Another thing is …
   6. Conclude:
      Finally, I'd like to say …
      Thank you all very much for listening to me.
      Are there any questions?

5. Mark pauses and words you want to stress. Practice reading it aloud to a partner. Give your talk to the class. Answer any questions.

Cheap Christopher

The title of my talk is "Cheap Christopher." That's what everyone calls my cousin. Why do they call him that? Well, simply because he's so stingy. He gets everything on the cheap. He's the stingiest person I've ever met, and that's why I want to talk about him today.

Let's start with some background. Christopher is intelligent. He's a part-time journalist and he's not poor at all. I think he makes about $50,000 a year. He's married with two children, and his wife has a good job, too. So why is Christopher so stingy?

First, let me tell you just how stingy he is. He never spends money on himself. He never buys new clothes. He gets them secondhand from thrift stores for about $5 an item. He never eats out in restaurants. When his work colleagues invite him out to lunch, he stays in his office and says he's expecting a phone call. He hardly ever uses his car. He says he can live on $10 a week. Can you believe that?

Another thing, Christopher never, ever invites friends to dinner, but he doesn't feel guilty about accepting their invitations. Do you know what he says? He says that they invite him to dinner just to have someone interesting to talk to.

All these things are pretty bad, but in my opinion the stingiest thing he's ever done is this. He went to a friend's wedding without a present. He just took some wrapping paper and a card saying "Love from Christopher" and put it on the table with the other presents. Afterwards he got a thank-you letter from the bride. She obviously thought she'd misplaced the present.

The obvious question is "why is he so stingy?" I asked him about it. He said, "I've always been stingy." When he was a child, he'd never buy his mother flowers on Mother's Day. He'd give her a bouquet from her own garden.

Finally, I'd like to say that Christopher may be the world's stingiest guy, but I still like him. Why, you may ask? Well, he's my cousin, and besides, he's got a lot of other good qualities, like his sense of humor. His wife doesn't seem to mind that he's so cheap. She says he's just "being careful with his money."

UNIT 10 FORMAL AND INFORMAL LETTERS AND E-MAILS—Do's and don'ts

1 You have looked at letters and e-mails in Units 1, 2, and 5. Are the following statements about **informal** letters and e-mails true or false? (Some are part true.)

1. You can begin with *Dear Rob*, *Hi Rob*, or just *Rob*.
2. Use contracted forms such as *won't*, *I've*, and *couldn't*.
3. The way you end the letter depends on how well you know the person.
4. You can end with *Good-bye*, *Bye for now*, *All the best*, *Best wishes*, *Take care*, *Yours*, or *Love*.
5. Sign or write your full name, and print it out underneath.
6. If you have forgotten to write something important, you can add it at the bottom with *PS*, for example, *PS Say Hi to Ellie! Tell her I'll be in touch*.

2 Are these statements about **formal** letters and e-mails true or false? (Some are part true.)

1. If you know the person's name, you can begin with *Dear Mr. Brown*, *Dear Robert Brown*, *Dear Brown*, *Dear Mr. Robert Brown*, or just *Brown*.
2. If you're writing to a woman, begin with *Dear Ms. Black*.
3. If you don't know their name, you can begin with *Dear Sir or Madam*.
4. Avoid contracted forms except *doesn't*, *don't*, or *didn't*.
5. If you begin with *Dear Sir or Madam*, end with *Yours faithfully* or just *Yours*. If you begin with the person's name, end with *Sincerely yours*.
6. Sign or write your full name.

3 Read the letter from Keiko to her friend, Amber Jones. Which parts sound too formal? Replace them with words on the right.

4 Write an informal letter to another student in the class (about 250 words). Ask a few questions about the other person's life, and then give some news about yourself. Invite the other person out, and give some suggestions for a time and place to meet.

4-2 Nagayama 3-chome
Tama-shi, Tokyo 206

Dear Ms. Jones,

How are things with you? I trust you and your family are in good health, and that you benefited from an enjoyable holiday in France. I recently went on a school trip for a few days. Please find enclosed a photo of me and several acquaintances at an ancient temple. Hope you like it.

I was most delighted to hear that you are coming to Japan in the near future! You didn't specify the exact dates. I would be grateful if you could supply them to me. I will do my utmost to ensure I have some time free in order to be able to accompany you around Tokyo. I can assure you that there is a lot to see and do here. We'll have lots of fun! The shops here are of a very high standard, too, so we'll no doubt end up buying excessive quantities of clothes!

In conclusion, I'm obliged to finish now. It's time for bed! Please contact me soon. I look forward to hearing from you.

Sincerely yours,

Keiko

PS Please give my sincere regards to your parents. Tell them I miss them!

Believe me,
had a great time
It's great news
hope
say when exactly
can't wait to hear
Anyway
Please let me know
Hi Amber!
get in touch
lots of
so I can show
soon
say hello
Love and best wishes
absolutely fantastic
a few friends
we're sure to
I'll do my best to make sure
I have to
I'm sending you
all well

UNIT 11 NARRATIVE WRITING 2—Linking words and expressions

1 Think of something that you looked forward to for a long time that finally happened.
- What was the occasion or event? Why did you want it so much?
- Did you have to make preparations for it? If so, what were they?
- What actually happened?
- Did it live up to your expectations or not?

Write some notes and then tell your partner about it.

2 Read these lines from Larry's story and reconstruct it with a partner.

> Larry's dream to fly airplanes / bought 20 balloons / a lawn chair / packed a few sandwiches and a BB gun / cut the rope / floated around / the winds were blowing / an American Airlines pilot at 3,500 meters / a helicopter / a TV reporter

3 Read the full story and compare it with yours. Match these five headings with the correct paragraphs.

- ☐ Serious problems
- ☐ Preparing for takeoff
- ☐ Down to earth with a bump
- ☐ Larry and his dream
- ☐ Flying high

4 Read the story again and complete it with a correct linking word or expression from the box.

| first of all   Finally   Eventually   Next |
| However   All day long   Then, one day |
| By this time   until   As soon as |
| Right away   Fortunately, just at that moment |
| Unfortunately   in order to   so   because |

5 Use your notes from Exercise 1 and write your story (about 250 words).

6 Read each other's stories and ask and answer questions about them.

Larry follows his dream

1. Larry was a truck driver, but his lifelong dream was to fly airplanes.
   (1)_____ he would watch the fighter jets criss-crossing the skies above his backyard and dream about the magic of flying. (2)_____, he had an idea. He drove to the nearest hardware store and bought 20 large balloons and five tanks of helium. (3)_____, they were not normal brightly colored party balloons but heavy one-meter weather balloons used by meteorologists.

2. Back in his yard, (4)_____, Larry used a rope to tie a chair to his car door. (5)_____ he tied the balloons to the chair and inflated them, one by one. (6)_____, he packed a few sandwiches and a bottle of Coke, loaded an BB gun, and climbed on to the chair. His plan was to float up lazily into the sky to about 60 meters, and then to pop a few balloons with the BB gun (7)_____ descend to earth again.

3. His preparations complete, Larry cut the rope. (8)_____, he didn't float up, he shot up, as if he had been fired from a cannon! Not to 60 meters, but up and up and up, (9)_____ about 3,500 meters. If he had popped any balloons at this height, he would have plummeted to earth, (10)_____ he just had to stay up there, floating around and wondering what to do.

4. (11)_____, night was falling and things were getting serious. Winds were blowing Larry out to sea. (12)_____ an amazed airline pilot spotted him and radioed the airport saying he'd just seen a man with a gun, sitting on a lawn chair at 3,500 meters. (13)_____ a helicopter was sent to rescue him, but it wasn't easy (14)_____ the wind from their rotor blades kept pushing the homemade airship further away. (15)_____, they managed to drop a line down from above, and pulled him to safety.

5. (16)_____ he was on the ground he was arrested. A TV reporter shouted, "Hey man, why did you do it?" Larry looked him in the eye, and said, "A man's got to follow his dreams."

UNIT 12 ADDING EMPHASIS IN WRITING—People of influence

1. Who are the most influential people in the world today? And in the past? Share ideas as a class.

2. Compare the two texts about Michelangelo. Work with a partner and find differences in the way the same information is presented.

   Find examples of how emphasis is added by:

   1. Changes of word order.
   2. Changes of words.
   3. Sentences that begin with *It was ...* and *What ...*.
   4. The use of *this* to refer back.

   Which text sounds better? Why?

3. Rephrase these sentences in different ways to make them more emphatic.

   1. I love my grandfather's kind, wrinkly smile.
      What I love about ...   *The thing I love about ...*
      What I love about my grandfather is his kind, wrinkly smile.
      The thing I love about my grandfather is his kind, wrinkly smile.
   2. They don't understand the president's policies.
      It's the president's policies ...   *What they ...*
   3. The softness of Norah Jones' voice makes it special.
      What makes ...   *It's the ...*
   4. I admired Mother Teresa's courage.
      What I admired about ...   *It was ...*
   5. The way Pele could head a soccer ball was amazing.
      What was ...   *What amazed me ...*

4. Research the career of someone you consider influential, e.g., an athlete, artist, singer, actor, writer, or businessperson.

   Using some of the structures for adding emphasis, write (about 250 words) about:

   - their early life
   - how their career grew
   - why he/she is/was a person of influence
   - the high points of their professional life

MICHELANGELO (1475–1564)

TEXT A

1. Michelangelo had a great influence on the world of art. He was a sculptor, an architect, a painter, and a poet.
2. He was born near Arezzo, but he considered Florence to be his hometown. He loved the city's art, architecture, and culture.
3. He concentrated on sculpture initially. He began to carve a figure of David from a huge block of marble in 1501. He finished it in 1504, when he was 29.
4. Pope Julius II asked him to paint the ceiling of the Sistine Chapel later. He worked at this every day for four years from 1508 till 1512. He lay on his back at the top of high scaffolding.
5. He designed many buildings. His greatest achievement as an architect was his work at St Peter's Basilica. Its revolutionary design is difficult to appreciate nowadays.
6. Michelangelo belongs to a small group of artists such as Shakespeare and Beethoven, who have been able to express humanity's deepest experiences through their work.

TEXT B

1. Michelangelo, sculptor, architect, painter, and poet, had a tremendous influence on the world of art.
2. Although he was born near Arezzo, it was Florence that he considered to be his hometown. What he loved above all about the city was its art, architecture, and culture.
3. Initially, he concentrated on sculpture. In 1501 he began to carve a figure of David from a huge block of marble. This he finished in 1504, when he was 29.
4. Later, he was asked by Pope Julius II to paint the ceiling of the Sistine Chapel. To do this, every day for four years, from 1508 till 1512, he worked lying on his back at the top of high scaffolding.
5. He designed many buildings, but it was his work at St Peter's Basilica that was his greatest achievement as an architect. What is difficult to appreciate nowadays is its revolutionary design.
6. There is a small group of artists such as Shakespeare and Beethoven, who, through their work, have been able to express the deepest experiences of humanity. Michelangelo belongs to this group.

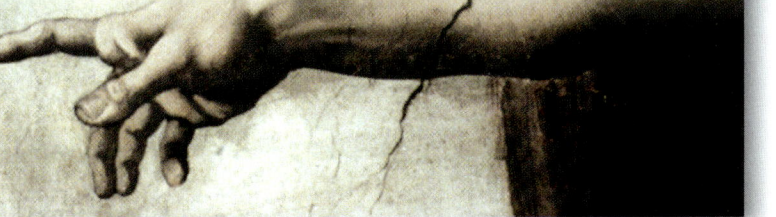

Tapescripts

UNIT 7

T 7.1

1. If I were you I wouldn't wear red. It doesn't suit you.
2. Is it OK if I make a suggestion?
3. You're allowed to smoke in the designated area only.
4. I'll be able to take you to the airport, after all.
5. You are required to obtain a visa to work in Australia.
6. It's always a good idea to make an appointment.
7. You're sure to pass. Don't worry.
8. You aren't permitted to walk on the grass.
9. I didn't manage to get through. The line was busy.
10. I refuse to discuss the matter any further.

T 7.2   See p. 58

T 7.3

1. **A** What the … where do you think you're going?
   B What do you mean?
   A Well, you're not allowed to turn right here.
   B Who says it's not allowed?
   A That sign does. "Do Not Enter." You ought to be able to read that.
   B Hey, it's impossible to see.
   A You'd better get you eyes tested. You're not fit to be on the roads.
2. **A** Promise not to tell anyone!
   B I promise.
   A It's really important not to tell a soul.
   B Trust me. I won't say a word.
   A But I know you. You're sure to tell someone.
   B Look. I really am able to keep a secret, you know. Oh, but is it OK if I tell David?
   A That's fine. He's invited too, of course. It's just that Ben and I want a really quiet affair, this being the second time around for both of us.

T 7.4

A I think you should swallow your pride and forgive and forget.
B Never! I will not.
A You'll have to in the end. You can't ignore each other forever.
B I might forgive him, but I can never forget.
A It must be possible to talk it over and work something out. You must for the sake of the children.
B Oh, I just don't know what to do!

T 7.5

A I don't know if I can come tonight.
B But you must. You said you would.
A Yeah, but I can't go out on weeknights. My parents won't let me.
B You could tell your parents that you're going over to the library to study.
A I can't. Somebody will see me and tell them.
B We'll have to cancel the party then. Lots of kids can't go out during final exams.

T 7.6

R Hello?
M Rebecca, Rebecca, is that you? I've got to talk to you.
R Maria, hi! Why all the excitement?
M Well, can you remember that quiz contest I entered, just for a laugh, a few weeks ago?
R Yes, I can. I remember you doing it in the coffee shop. It was the one in the *Post*, wasn't it? Didn't you have to name a bunch of capital cities?
M Yes, that's it. You've got it. Well, get this, I *won*! I came in first!
R No way! I don't believe it! What's the prize?
M A trip to New York.
R You must be kidding! That's great! For how long?
M Just three days—but it's three days in the Ritz Carlton, of all places!
R Well, you should be able to do quite a lot in three days. And the Ritz Carlton! I'm impressed! Doesn't that overlook Central Park?
M Yes, it does.
R I thought so. Can't say I've been there, of course.
M Well, you can now!
R What do you mean? How would I ever be able to?
M Well, it's a trip for two and I'd really love it if you would come with me. Will you?
R You can't be serious! You know I'd love to! But why me? Surely you should be taking David.
M Haven't you heard? David and I broke up.
R Oh, I'm sorry! I didn't know. When did this happen?
M Well, a couple of weeks ago. We hadn't been getting along for a long time. Anyway, you've got to come with me!
R Well, what can I say? How could I possibly refuse an offer like that?
M You'll come then?
R I definitely will.

T 7.7

I = Interviewer, P = Pratima
I How old were you when you met your husband, Pratima?
P Mmm …. I was just sixteen.
I Were you still at school?
P No, I'd left school but I was having private tuition at home, to prepare me for some exams.
I And your father arranged your marriage, is that right?
P That's right.
I Could you tell me how he did that?
P Well, he looked around for a suitable husband. He asked friends and relatives if they knew anyone, and found out about their education, their background and um most importantly the family's background. He managed to get a lot of information about them, you know.
I And how long did this take?
P Not too long in my case, but you know um sometimes a father can see up to a hundred men before he chooses one. For my sister, my elder sister he saw over one hundred men before …
I He saw how many? Goodness. It must take up a lot of time.
P Yes, it can be difficult to decide but for me he saw only two um … one in the morning and one in the afternoon and um he chose the second one.
I What a day! Can you tell me about it?
P Yes … well, in the morning the first man was very wealthy, and he was well-dressed and um had good manners but um he hadn't had a good education.
I Ah. And the other one?
P Well, he wasn't terribly wealthy, but he was well-educated and he came from a good background um his family owned a village and were like princes. He was 22 and studying law.
I And this one um your father chose?
P That's right. I think he thought money wasn't everything—for my father education was more important and anyway, if a man is well-educated he will earn in the end. Actually, Shyam, that's my husband's name, Shyam didn't want to get married at all but his father had told him he must, so when he came to my house to meet my father, he was very badly-dressed because he hoped my father would refuse him. But luckily for me my father did like him, and, uh, he had to say yes.
I He had to?
P Oh yes, he had promised his father.
I And what about you? Did you meet both men?
P Yes, I met them that day. First my family spoke to them and then they called me in and we um spoke for four … four or five minutes.
I And did you prefer the second?
P Well, actually I wasn't sure. I left it to my father.
I You must trust him a lot.
P Oh, yes.
I So what happened next?
P Well, after a while, there was a special day when I went to meet his family and his family came to meet mine. It was kind of an engagement party. But we—you know—Shyam and me, we used to be on the phone every day and we'd meet regularly but always we had to have a chaperone. And after ten months we got married.
I And how long have you been married?
P Nearly twenty-five years now.
I And ….it's been a successful marriage? Your father made a good choice?
P Oh… yes, of course and we have two beautiful sons. They're twenty-two and seventeen now.
I And will you arrange their marriages?
P Oh yes. My husband is planning them now. He's been asking families for some time already and …
I And your sons want it?
P Well, Krishna, he's the eldest, he's OK about it— he's studying hard and hasn't got the time to meet girls but…
I Yes, what about the youngest? Ravi, isn't it?
P Yes um, well actually, Ravi's not so keen. It might be difficult to persuade …
I But you still believe that the system of arranged marriages is a good one?
P Oh yes, I do, of course I do—but you know it depends on a lot, uh, especially on the family choosing the right person. But one main reason, I think it does work, is that the couple enter the marriage not *expecting* too much, if you see what I mean. Actually, you know, there are many more divorces between couples who thought they were marrying for love. You know my mother um she had to marry at thirteen but she's still happily married nearly fifty years later. Of course, nowadays thirteen is considered too young but you know… times change.
I Yeah, that's very true. Thank you very much indeed Pratima.

T 7.8

1. **A** My friends went to Alaska on vacation.
   B They went *where*?
2. **A** I got home at 5:00 this morning.
   B You got home *when*?
3. **A** I paid $300 for a pair of jeans.
   B You paid *how much*?
4. **A** I met the president while I was out shopping.
   B You met *who*?
5. **A** He invited me to the White House for lunch.
   B He invited you *where*?

T 7.9

1. **A** I'm dying for a cup of coffee.
   B I wouldn't mind one myself.
2. **A** His parents are pretty well off, aren't they?
   B You can say that again! They're totally loaded!
3. **A** You must have hit the roof when she told you she'd crashed your car.
   B Well, yeah, I was a little upset.
4. **A** I think Tony was a little rude last night.
   B No kidding! He was completely out of line!
5. **A** I can't stand the sight of him!
   B I have to say I'm not too big on him, either.
6. **A** He isn't very smart, is he?
   B That's for sure. He's as dumb as dirt.
7. **A** I'm fed up with this weather! It's freezing.
   B I guess it is a little chilly.
8. **A** Well, that was a fantastic trip!
   B Yes, it was a nice little break, but all good things must come to an end.
9. **A** I'm wiped out. I've got to go to bed.
   B Yeah. I'm a little tired, too.
10. **A** They're obviously madly in love.
    B Yeah, they do seem to get along well.

T 7.10   See p. 65

T 7.11

1. **A** Is that a new watch? I bet that cost something.
   B Something? It cost a fortune!
2. **A** It's a little chilly in here, don't you think?
   B You can say that again. I'm absolutely freezing.
3. **A** These shoes aren't bad, are they?
   B They're *gorgeous*! I want them!
4. **A** Can we pull over at the next rest stop? I could use something to eat.
   B Me too. I'm starving. I didn't have breakfast this morning.

UNIT 8

T 8.1

Welcome to JUMBOLAIR, Florida—the world's only housing development where the super-rich can commute to work by jet plane from their own front doors.
Jumbolair's most famous resident is Hollywood movie star John Travolta, whose $3.5 million mansion is big enough to park a row of airplanes, including a Gulfstream executive jet, a two-seater jet fighter, and a four-engine Boeing 707, previously owned by Frank Sinatra. Travolta holds a commercial pilot's license, which means he's qualified to fly passenger jets. He can land his planes and taxi them up to his front gates. His sumptuous Florida home, which is built in the style of an airport terminal building, is the ultimate boys' fantasy house made real. As well as the parking lots for the jets, there is a heliport, swimming pool and gym, stables for 75 horses, and of course a 1.4-mile runway. Family man Travolta, who lives with wife Kelly, daughter Ella Bleu, and aptly named son Jett, flies daily from his home when filming. Walking out of his door and into the cockpit, he is airborne in minutes. His neighbors, most of whom share his love of aviation, don't seem to mind the roar of his jets. They say that it's nice to meet a superstar who isn't full of himself. "He's just a regular guy, very friendly," says one neighbor.

T 8.2

1. The area of New York I like best is Soho.
2. My father, who's a doctor, plays the drums.
3. The book that I'm reading now is fascinating.
4. Paul passed his driver's test on the first try, which surprised everybody.
5. People who smoke risk getting all sorts of illnesses.
6. I met a man whose main aim in life was to visit every capital city in the world.
7. The Channel Tunnel, which opened in 1995, is a great way to get from England to France.
8. What I like best about work are the vacation days.
9. A short bald man seen running away from the scene of the crime is being sought by the police.

T 8.3

1. **A** How did you do on the math test?
   B Oh! Don't ask! It's too awful.
   A Oh, man. What did you get?
   B Twenty-two percent. I came in last and I thought I was going to do really well.
2. **A** How was your vacation?
   B Great, thanks. Just what we needed.
   A Did you do much?
   B Not a lot. We just sat by the pool, read books, and took it easy for two whole weeks. Absolute bliss.
3. **A** Have you heard about Dave and Maggie?
   B No. Tell me, tell me!
   A Well, last week they went to a party, had this huge fight in front of all these people and … .
   B Did it get physical?
   A Oh yeah! Maggie shoved Dave into a flowerpot, told him to get lost, and went off with another guy!
   B What? I'm amazed! I just can't believe Maggie'd do such a thing. It doesn't sound like her at all.
4. **A** Come on in. You must be exhausted!
   B Oof, I am. I've been traveling for the past 30 hours and I haven't slept a wink.
   A I know—I can never sleep on a plane, either. Just sit down, take it easy, and I'll get you some water.
5. **A** How's the new job going?
   B Good, thanks, very good—but it's quite difficult. I have to deal with so many new things. Still, I'm enjoying it all.
   A Mmm—I know what you mean.
   B Yeah. It's great to be doing something that's so satisfying. And I love meeting so many people from abroad.
   A Absolutely.
6. **A** So anyway, just to end the perfect evening, I had to walk back home because I'd lost the car keys and I didn't have any money for a taxi. I didn't get home until three in the morning.
   B That's the funniest thing I've heard for ages. Poor you. Sorry I'm laughing.
   A Well, I'm glad you think it's so funny—I didn't think it was funny at the time.
7. **A** There is just nothing good on TV tonight!
   B What about that wildlife program?
   A Do you mean the one about the life of frogs?
   B Yeah—does it look any good?
   A You're kidding. It looks totally boring.
8. **A** What's the matter with you?
   B Oh my gosh—I just put my foot right in my mouth.
   A What do you mean?
   B Well, I was talking to that lady over there and I asked her when her baby was due, and, um, she told me she wasn't pregnant.
   A Oh, no! That's awful!

T 8.4

Lost in her thoughts, a beautiful young woman was sitting in her country garden, watching a bee lazily going from rose to rose gathering honey.

T 8.5

1. Exhausted after a hard day's work, a balding, middle-aged man wearing a rumpled suit, and carrying a briefcase, walked slowly along the road that led from the station to his home, pausing only to look up at the night sky.
2. Peter, who's very wealthy, has a huge, 16th-century farmhouse, surrounded by woods in the heart of the English countryside.
3. Ann Croft, the world famous actress, who married for the sixth time only last month, was seen having an intimate lunch in a Los Angeles restaurant with a man who was definitely not her husband.
4. The trip to Hawaii, which we had looked forward to so much, was a complete and utter disaster from start to finish.
5. A ten-year-old boy, walking home from school, found an old, battered, leather wallet filled with $5,000 in $50 bills on Main Street.

T 8.6   Simone

Well, it was when I was living in Cairo. And it was in the middle of the summer, so it was extremely hot, between 40 and 45 degrees centigrade, and, um, stupidly we decided to go dancing. And, um, we went to this nightclub, and we must have danced for hours and hours. It was very hot inside and we were sweating profusely, and by the time we came out it was about 5 o'clock in the morning, and we decided, "Ooh, wouldn't it be a great idea to go to the pyramids and see the sunrise?"
So we jumped in a taxi and the taxi was quite stuffy and hot, um and we must have been starting to dehydrate at this point. Anyway, we got to the pyramids, and the sun was just starting to come up. And in Egypt, as soon as the sun comes up the temperature rises dramatically. But we were so excited at seeing the pyramids that we decided just to, um, to go and walk and see.
At this point, um, a man approached us and asked us if we wanted to borrow his motorcycle, or rent his motorcycle, and we said yes. So my friend and I, we jumped onto the motorcycle and raced out into the desert, only to find after about ten, fifteen minutes, that the motorcycle was pretty old and suddenly it broke down! So we were miles from anywhere and had to push this motorcycle to get back. I was the one at the back pushing the motorcycle and of course I was using lots of energy. I was losing a lot of fluid. And it was getting hotter and hotter. Anyway, by the time we got home, um, I did start to feel a bit strange, I had a slight headache and, um, I decided to go straight to bed. Anyway, I woke up about half an hour later, feeling pretty confused, and sick, a little nauseous. And I realized that my brain wasn't working properly, and that in fact I probably had heat exhaustion. Anyway, it wasn't very pleasant and, uh, it was a lesson in what not to do in temperatures like that. I've never done that again. And I always carry my salt tablets with me now.

T 8.7 Anna

The time that I was very, very cold um was a time when I was working in Russia, in a small town in central Russia, and I was going to see some friends who lived on the outskirts of the town. And they were worried about me getting lost and they said that they'd come to the tram stop to meet me. But I wanted to be independent, so I told them, "Don't be silly, of course I'll find it."

And on the day of the visit, um, it was very, very cold. It might have been minus 30, but it might have been colder than that. And, um, it was, it was so cold that at some of the tram stops and bus stops there were bonfires lit—special street fires um to keep people warm. And I think it was a day when the schools were closed, and the children didn't go to school because it was so cold. So I put on all the clothes that I had, all the scarves and sweaters, and I took the tram to the outskirts of the town where my friends lived. And I got off the tram, which was heated, into this cold white world. And um, it was so cold that when you breathed in, little balls of ice formed in your nostrils. You had to keep your scarf over your mouth and nose.

About a minute, two minutes after getting off the tram my feet and hands were already hurting they were so cold. So I was walking around, trying to find the house, but it was completely anonymous this, this landscape. There were these huge snow-covered white blocks, these buildings, fifteen or sixteen floors, but they all looked exactly the same. And I couldn't find the name of the street either, and it was very, very quiet, and the tram had gone. Um… and I began, actually, to get very frightened because I was feeling so, so cold. Um, my feet and hands had gone beyond hurting almost, I couldn't feel them any more. Um, it was pretty difficult to breathe because of the icy scarf over my mouth and nose. I just couldn't find where they lived! And I asked an old lady the way but my Russian wasn't good enough. She didn't understand me. And I was beginning to really, seriously panic when suddenly, in the distance, I saw my friends. They'd come to find me and they took me home.

T 8.8

1. We went dancing in temperatures of over 40°C, which was a pretty stupid thing to do.
2. My friends were worried I'd get lost, which was understandable.
3. We visited the pyramids at sunrise, which was just amazing.
4. My nostrils actually froze, which is hard to believe.
5. This motorcycle broke down, which was no joke.
6. The old lady didn't understand a word I said, which is hardly surprising since my Russian's lousy.

T 8.9

1. A Did you get very cold in that snowstorm?
   B Snowstorm! It was a blizzard! We're absolutely freezing!
2. A I bet you were pretty excited when your team won.
   B Excited! We were absolutely thrilled!
3. A I thought she looked kind of silly in that flowery hat, didn't you?
   B Silly? She looked absolutely ridiculous!
4. A Come on, nobody'll notice that tiny pimple on your nose.
   B They will, I just know they will! It's absolutely enormous!
5. A I thought the last episode of *Friends* was absolutely hilarious.
   B Mmm. I wouldn't say that. It was pretty funny but not hilarious.
6. A Len left early. He wasn't feeling well.
   B I'm not surprised. When I saw him this morning he looked absolutely awful!

T 8.10 See p. 72

T 8.11 See p. 72

T 8.12

I am absolutely amazed and delighted to receive this award. I'm truly grateful to all those wonderful people who voted for me. *Red Hot in the Snow* was an absolutely fantastic movie to act in, not only because of all the totally brilliant and talented people involved in the making of it, but also because of the fabulous, thrilling, and often extremely dangerous locations in Alaska. None of us could have predicted that it would be such a huge success. My special thanks go to Marius Aherne, my excellent director; Lulu Lovelace, my gorgeous costar; Roger Sims, for writing a script that was both fascinating and hilarious; and last but not least to my marvelous wife, Glynis, for her priceless support. I absolutely adore you all.

T 8.13

1. A Hello. Could I make an appointment for our golden retriever, Molly?
   B Sure. What seems to be the problem?
   A Well, she's stopped eating her food, which is very unusual for her, and she has no interest in going out for walks. She just lies around all day long …
2. A What have we got here?
   B All these old bottles, a washing machine that doesn't work anymore, and a whole bunch of cardboard.
   A All right, well the bottles can go in there with the glass. And the washing machine—that would be metal, so it goes over there…
3. A Hello. I'd like to open an account, please.
   B Are you a student?
   A Yes, I am.
   B Well, we have a couple of special accounts for students. One gives you free checking and ATM access with a minimum balance of $1000. Another gives you up to ten transactions per month with no minimum balance, and a monthly fee of …
4. A Yes, please. How can I help you?
   B Yeah, I'm driving cross-country this summer, to help my grandma move, and I want some kind of coverage in case the car breaks down.
   A I see. Well, you could get a year's membership, and that includes free towing anywhere in the US. Just call this number if you have car trouble, and we'll send someone to tow you to the nearest garage.
   B Sounds good. How much does that cost?
   A It's $65 for a year, and your membership card can get you discounts on hotels, airfare, restaurants…
5. A Hello there, can I help you?
   B Yes, I'm looking for something for a leaky faucet? The water keeps drip, drip, dripping all night!
   A Aw, sounds terrible.
   B Yeah. My roommate said we need to replace some kind of seal, or gasket? Some kind of rubber thing, I guess.
   A I know just what you need. Follow me and I'll show you…

UNIT 9

T 9.1

Dear Sally,
I'm sending this through classmates.com. Do you remember me? We used to go to Springfield East together. You were the first person I got to know when I started there.
We used to sit next to each other in class, but then the teachers made us sit apart because we were always giggling so much.
I remember we'd go back to your house after school every day and listen to music for hours on end. We'd get all the Beatles records as soon as they came out. Once we ate all the food in your fridge and your mother was furious.
Do you remember that time we nearly blew up the science lab? The teacher went crazy, but it wasn't our fault. We used to call him "Mickey Mouse" because he had sticky-out ears.
I still see Penny, and she's still as wild as ever. We meet up every now and then, and we'll always end up chatting about old times together. She's always talking about a class reunion. So if you're interested, drop me a line.
Looking forward to hearing from you.
Your old friend,
Alison Wright
PS I'm not used to calling you Sally Davis! To me, you're still Sally Wilkinson!

T 9.2

we used to go to school together
we used to sit next to each other
we were always giggling so much
we'd go back to your house
we used to call him "Mickey Mouse"
I'm not used to calling you Sally Davis.

T 9.3

1. I got along very well with my mother. She was my best friend, still is. We had to get along, really. Dad left when I was three. I used to tell her everything, well, nearly everything. And she'd talk to me very openly, too. Sometimes she'd say to me, "Don't go to school today. Stay with me." And we'd go out shopping or something like that. It's a wonder I had any education at all, the number of days I missed from school.
2. I don't remember much about my childhood. My wife's always asking me questions like "When you were a boy, did you used to …?" and I reply, "I don't know. I can't remember." We didn't … uh … really, we didn't use to talk very much. We weren't very close, or if we were we didn't show it. I remember I used to have my hair cut every Friday. My father was in the Army, and he had a thing about short hair, so every week he'd take me to the barber. I had the shortest hair in the school. I used to hate it. And him.
3. I'm not a very neat person, but my mother's a real clean freak, so she's always telling me to pick things up and put them away, and do this and do that. She'll go on for hours about how "Cleanliness is next to godliness," and that just makes me want to scream. My father isn't like that at all. He's much more laid back. I think he's just learned to screen out my mother.
4. I have very fond memories of my childhood. To me it represented security. We used to do a lot together as a family. I remember walks, and picnics, and going for car rides on a Sunday afternoon. Every Friday when my Dad came home, he'd bring us each a treat, just something little. My mother used to say he was spoiling us, but why not? It didn't do us any harm.

T 9.4

1. A You don't like your new teacher, do you?
   B Not a lot, but we're getting used to her.
2. A How can you get up at five o'clock in the morning?
   B No problem. I'm used to it.
3. A How come you know Mexico City so well?
   B I used to live there.
4. A How are you finding your new job?
   B Difficult, but I'm getting used to it bit by bit.
5. A Do you read comics?
   B I used to when I was young, but not anymore.
6. A You two argue so much. How can you live together?

B After 20 years of marriage we're used to each other.

T 9.5

1. Alan
I was very fortunate in high school to have a really good teacher for a subject called social studies, which combines history and geography. And I think the thing that made this teacher so good was that he not only had a terrific sense of humor, but he could also keep the class under control. We always paid attention when he wanted us to pay attention, but he could always get us to laugh at the same time. So he had a way of kind of being flexible in his teaching style. And he'd do crazy things like, you know, sometimes he'd stand on a desk and recite a poem, or he'd draw funny pictures on the blackboard. But I never forgot him. His name was Mr. Sparks, which I think is a fantastic name for a teacher. And he'd stand at the front of the class—he had this sort of funny beard—a short, pointy beard, and glasses. And this kind of graying, slicked back hair. And he'd stand there and look at us with this terrifying look on his face, and then tell a joke! Just to make us all laugh!

2. John
I had a teacher at school who was just awful. He taught French and German, and his name was Colin Tivvy. I'll never forget that name. It sends shivers down my spine just to hear it. It wasn't that he was a bad teacher. In fact he used to get very good results. It was the way he got those results. He taught out of pure fear. All the kids were scared stiff of him, so you'd do his homework first and best, because the last thing you wanted was to make a mistake. If you made any mistake, in homework or in class, you had to write it out one hundred times that night. He'd been a soldier in the army, and he'd worked as an interrogator, and that was just how he taught. We had to stand in a line outside his classroom, and when he was ready, he'd shout, "Get in, men!," and we'd all march into class. And all through the class, he'd pace up and down the classroom, and he used to wear those kind of shoes that didn't make a noise, you know? And the worst feeling in the whole world was when you knew he was just behind you. You were waiting for a smack on the back of the head. But the worst was when he picked you up by the hairs on the back of your neck. That hurt.

3. Liz
The teacher I remember most from my school days was a teacher named Miss Potts. She was a history teacher and I was about thirteen or fourteen years old. We were all very interested in fashion, and Miss Potts used to wear the most amazing things to come in to teach. She was a very memorable teacher. Every day we'd be asking ourselves, "What's she gonna wear today?" She would wear blue tights with red skirts and very red sweaters, and very bright red lipstick, and she'd come teetering into the classroom on very high heels, and we thought she looked wonderful. But the very best thing about Miss Potts was the way she actually taught history—it's what makes her most memorable. She not only brought history to life, but she made it seem easy. The way she described the characters from history made us feel as if we knew them. And sometimes instead of writing essays we would do little cartoon strips of the different tales from history, and we loved it. And she always encouraged you, even if your answer was dead wrong.

She was a brilliant, brilliant teacher. It's interesting 'cause I think another teacher who was named Miss Potts would probably have been called "potty" or um given some nickname like that, but there was something about her that we respected so much that she just never had a nickname.

4. Kate
My favorite is named Mr. Brown. We call him Brownie, but not to his face. We wouldn't dare. He's my homeroom teacher, and he's great. He'll joke and make fun of you, but never in a horrible, nasty way. And we like to pull his leg, too. You know, he's bald, poor guy, totally bald, but when it's his birthday we'll ask him if he wants a comb or a brush, or something like that. But there's a line we all know we can't cross. We have a lot of respect for him as a teacher, and he treats us totally fairly, but he also keeps his distance. He never tries to be one of us. If a teacher ever tries to be, you know, a teenager like us, same music, same clothes, same jokes, it just doesn't work. But there's another side to Brownie. He's also in charge of discipline at the school, so whenever a student, you know, misbehaves or mouths off to a teacher, they get sent to Mr. Brown and he scares the pants off them. And when he shouts, boy he is absolutely terrifying. No one, but no one, messes with Mr. Brown.

T 9.6
Theme song to *Friends*

T 9.7
1. I like her because she's so different from the others. She thinks differently, she behaves differently. She'll say the craziest things in the most serious way.
2. I like him because he's so cute and so amazingly self-centered. He's so uncomplicated. What you see is what you get. So charmingly dumb and unsophisticated.
3. I can't stand her because she's so fussy and uptight. She has to have control over everything and everybody. And she screeches.
4. He really annoys me because he's so hopeless with women. But he's so funny. He uses his humor and sarcasm as a defense mechanism to get out of trouble. How he ended up with Monica, I'll never know.
5. She's my favorite because she's incredibly good-looking. She's a bit scatter-brained. She's always losing things. She's a real daddy's girl. She was so popular in high school.
6. He's my favorite because he's always falling in love with the wrong woman. He's the coolest of the non-cool crowd. He's so sensible, and his parents think he can do no wrong, but he's always getting into trouble.

T 9.8
where   nose   mail   break   through   sent

T 9.9 See p. 80

T 9.10
Customer Waiter! I'm in a hurry. Will my pizza be long?
Waiter No, sir. It'll be round!

What's the difference between a sailor and someone who goes shopping?
One goes to sail the seas, the other goes to see the sales.

What's the difference between a jeweler and a jailer?
One sells watches and the other watches cells.

T 9.11

1. Vicky
If you ask me, this is a terrible idea. Firstly, it would be an infringement on individual freedom. Secondly, another way of saying fast food is convenience food, and that means it really suits the kind of lifestyle of people today. Another thing is that it would be a tax on people who are less well off. Personally, I don't eat in these places, but that's not the point. The point I'm trying to make is that people should be allowed to eat what they want.

2. Al
To tell you the truth, I haven't really thought about it. I suppose the problem is that we don't know what's in these burgers and pizzas. As far as I'm concerned, people can do what they want. I don't see what's wrong with that. Actually, I'm seeing a friend for lunch and we're going to have a burger. There's that new place that just opened, you know, down by the square. It's supposed to be pretty good. Anyway, as I was saying, I don't really feel strongly one way or the other.

3. Beth-Anne
If you want my opinion, I think this is a really good idea. There are far too many people who have a terrible diet, and they just go to the nearest hamburger joint and fill themselves up with junk. Basically, it's laziness. As I understand it, they just can't be bothered to buy fresh food and cook it. But the main point is that fast food, or junk food, is too cheap. If it was taxed, people would think twice before buying it. What really worries me is that the next generation is going to have so many problems with kids being overweight.

T 9.12
If you ask me …
Another thing is that …
That's not the point.
The point I'm trying to make is that …
To tell you the truth …
I suppose the problem is that …
As far as I'm concerned …
Anyway, as I was saying …
If you want my opinion …
As I understand it …
But the main point is that …
What really worries me is that …

T 9.13 See p. 122

UNIT 10

T 10.1
1. She must have been very rich.
2. I had to do my homework.
3. I couldn't sleep because of the noise.
4. They can't have been in. There were no lights on.
5. I thought that was Jane but I might have been wrong.
6. You should have seen a doctor.

T 10.2
A You know that prehistoric man, the one they discovered in Italy years ago …
B You mean that guy in the Alps?
A Yeah, that's the one. He's supposed to be about 5,000 years old. They've done all sorts of tests on him, you know DNA tests and stuff, to find out about his life.
B What was he? Some sort of hunter?
A Well, they aren't sure. He could have been a hunter, or he could have been some kind of shepherd, you know, looking after his sheep up in the mountains. The mystery is, what was he doing up there? He might just have gotten lost for all we know.

B It must have been cold up there. How did he keep warm?
A I guess he lived in a cave and wore stuff like animal skins. They think he fell asleep while he was taking shelter from a snowstorm, so he may have died from cold and starvation. He shouldn't have gone up so high without the right, you know, protective clothing.
B I wonder what they did for food 5,000 years ago. They hunted wild animals, didn't they, with arrows and axes and things?
A Yeah, I guess they ate a lot of meat, and berries and fruit. They might have even grown crops, you know, like grains to make bread.
B No, they can't have been that clever. I bet they didn't know how to do that. I'd have thought they just ate meat, you know, like carnivores.
A Who knows? Maybe these tests will tell us. I figure they didn't get around much. It would have been too difficult.
B Sure. I wouldn't have thought they traveled much at all. I bet they stayed in the same area. How old was he when he died?
A They think he was maybe 40 to 45, which must have been pretty old in those days.
B I bought that magazine, *New Scientist*, so we can read all about the results.
A You shouldn't have bothered. I downloaded them from the Internet. Let's take a look at them.

T 10.3

1. What was he?
   He could have been a hunter, or he could have been a shepherd.
2. What was he doing in the mountains?
   He might have been looking after his sheep, or he might have gotten lost.
3. Where did he live? What did he wear?
   He must have lived in a cave. He must have worn animal skins.
4. How did he die?
   He may have fallen asleep. He may have died of cold and starvation.
5. Was it a good idea to go so high?
   He shouldn't have gone so high on his own. He should have worn protective clothing.
6. What did he eat?
   He must have eaten a lot of meat and berries. They might have grown crops like grains to make bread.
   They can't have grown crops. I'd have thought they just ate meat.
7. Did they travel much?
   I wouldn't have thought they traveled much at all.
   They must have stayed in the same area.
8. How old was he when he died?
   He could have been between 40 and 45. That must have been pretty old in those days.

T 10.4

1. I *did* tell you about Joe's party. You must not have been listening.
2. Thanks so much for all your help. I couldn't have managed without you.
3. Flowers, for me! Oh, that's so kind, but you really shouldn't have.
4. Come on! We're only five minutes late. The movie may not have started yet.
5. I don't believe that Kathy's going out with Mark. She would have told me, I know she would.
6. We raced to get to the airport on time, but we shouldn't have worried. The flight was delayed.
7. We've got a letter here that isn't for us. The mailman must have delivered it by mistake.
8. You shouldn't have gone swimming in such rough seas. You could have drowned!

T 10.5

Hello?
Oh, it's you.
We're all right, no thanks to you. Why are you calling?
What do you mean, next Saturday? What about next Saturday?
Already! Is it the second Saturday of the month so soon? Yes, I suppose it is. All right, then.
Where are you thinking of taking them? The children always pester me if they don't know, especially Daniel.
The zoo! Again! Can't you think of anything else? They hated it last time. Nicky did, anyway.
That's not what she told me. Anyway, that's up to you. What time are you going to pick them up?
OK. I'll have them ready. By the way, when they come home after a day with you, they're always filthy. Can't Alison wash their clothes?
Well, she has enough time to go shopping and have lunch with her friends, from what the kids have told me.
All right! I don't want to argue about it.
I'll tell them you called. Bye.

T 10.6

Hello?
This is Jeremy Brook speaking.
Sorry—Janice who?
I'm sorry. I don't think I know anyone by that name.
On vacation? Did we? When was that?
In Greece! Of course! I remember! You're the girl who was in the next room. That was years ago! How are you?
I'm fine. What a surprise! What are you doing? Where are you?
Here? What are you doing here?
Um … well … I'd love to, but uh … well, it's not very convenient, actually.
Yes, I know I said that, but that was a long time ago, and um … our apartment isn't that big, and uh…
Yes, I am. I got married last year.
Well, I'm glad you understand. I'm sorry to let you down. I'd have liked to help, but you see what I mean.
Maybe we could meet for a drink … you know, for old times' sake?
No, I suppose you're right. Well, it was nice to hear your voice again. Enjoy yourself here in California.
Thanks. Bye, Janice. Same to you.

T 10.7

1. **A** That exam was totally impossible!
   B You can say that again! I couldn't possibly have passed.
2. **A** You might as well apply for the job, even though you're too young.
   B Yes, why not! After all, I've got nothing to lose. You never know, I might be just the person they're looking for.
3. I know I shouldn't have eaten a whole tub of ice cream, but I just couldn't help it. I feel as fat as a pig now.
4. **A** I'm going to tell her exactly what I think of her.
   B I wouldn't do that if I were you. It could get really nasty.
5. **A** You should have told me that Jackie and Dave broke up!
   B Sorry! I thought you knew. Everybody else does.
6. **A** I think you should forget all about her and move on.
   B Believe me, I would if I could. But I just can't get her out of my mind. I think it must be love.
   A Oh no!
7. **A** You should have been here yesterday! You'd have died laughing!
   B Why? What was so funny?
   B Pedro was imitating the teacher, and he was so good, when the teacher walked in.
8. **A** Then I found out that Annie's been going out with … guess who? Dave!
   B Duh! I could have told you *that*. It's common knowledge. Where have you been?
9. I'd known this guy for five minutes when he asked me to marry him! I just couldn't believe it! Maybe he does that to every girl he meets.
10. **A** I could use a break.
    B Me, too. I'm dying for some coffee. This class has been going on forever.

T 10.8

Jim, who ran away from his nurse, and was eaten by a lion

There was a boy whose name was Jim;
His friends were very good to him.
They gave him tea, and cakes, and jam,
And slices of delicious ham,
And read him stories through and through,
And even took him to the zoo—
But there it was the dreadful fate
Befell him, I now relate.
You know—at least you ought to know,
For I have often told you so—
That children never are allowed
To leave their nurses in a crowd;
Now this was Jim's especial foible,
He ran away when he was able,
And on this inauspicious day
He slipped his hand and ran away!
He hadn't gone a yard when—bang!
With open jaws, a lion sprang,
And hungrily began to eat
The boy: beginning at his feet.
Now just imagine how it feels
When first your toes and then your heels,
And then by gradual degrees,
Your shins and ankles, calves and knees,
Are slowly eaten, bit by bit.
No wonder Jim detested it!
No wonder that he shouted "Hi!"
The honest keeper heard his cry,
Though very fat, he almost ran
To help the little gentleman.
"Ponto!" he cried, with angry frown
"Let go, sir! Down, sir! Put it down!"
The lion having reached his head
The miserable boy was dead!
When nurse informed his parents they
Were more concerned than I can say.
His mother, as she dried her eyes,
Said, "Well—it gives me no surprise,
He would not do as he was told!"
His father, who was self-controlled
Bade all the children round attend
To James' miserable end,
And always keep a-hold of nurse
For fear of finding something worse.

T 10.9

1. **A** How's the new job?
   B OK. My boss seemed very strict at first, but underneath it all she's very kind and generous. She understands the retail business very well, so she knows what she's doing.
2. **A** Can you help me with my computer? I can't open any of my files.
   B Listen, you'd better accept the reality that your computer is ancient. It's been about to stop working for years. You can get a new one for about $500 these days.
   A Are you joking?
   B No, I'm perfectly serious.
3. **A** Pat's been unbearable lately. That promotion has made her feel more important than she is. She's been shouting at everyone. She's always spoken in a harsh and unkind way, but now she's upsetting everyone.
   B I know. I'll have to talk to her honestly and openly.

T 10.10

1. **A** How's the new job?
   B OK. My boss seemed very strict at first, but underneath it all she's got a heart of gold. She has a good head for the retail business, so she knows what she's doing.
2. **A** Can you give me a hand with my computer? I can't open any of my files.
   B Listen, you'd better face the fact that your computer is ancient. It's been on its last legs for years. You can get a new one for about $500 these days.
   A Are you pulling my leg?
   B No, I'm perfectly serious.
3. **A** Pat's been unbearable lately. That promotion has gone to her head. She's been shouting at everyone. She's always had a sharp tongue, but now she's upsetting everyone.
   B I know. I'll have to have a heart-to-heart talk with her.

UNIT 11

T 11.1

1. It's raining again. I wish it wasn't.
2. I'm not going out tonight. I wish I was.
3. There's nothing good on TV. I wish there was.
4. I don't like my job. I wish I did.
5. My boyfriend and I broke up last week. I wish we hadn't.
6. I know he won't call me. I wish he would.
7. I feel really depressed. I wish I didn't.
8. I can't talk to anyone about it. I wish I could.

T 11.2

1. **A** No, I can't possibly go out tonight. I shouldn't have gone out last night.
   B Come on—we had a great time. It was a wild party!
   A I know it was.
   B So, when's your exam?
   A Tomorrow, 9 o'clock. If only I hadn't left *all* my studying till the last minute.
   B I wouldn't worry if I were you. You know you always do OK.
   A There's always a first time.
   B Good luck anyway.
2. **A** If only we could just fly off to that island.
   B That would be fantastic. I'd sit on a beach and read all day.
   A I'd just sleep forever. I can't remember the last time I got a full night's sleep.
   B Yeah. Sometimes I wish I'd never had kids. I mean, not *really*, but—
   A I know what you mean. No—you can't have an ice cream cone. I said no!
3. **A** Oh, man! What would you give to drive one of those?
   B Which one would you choose if you had the money?
   A That's a big "if"! But … mmm … if I won the lottery, I'd buy the Aston Martin.
   B I wouldn't—I'd go for the Ferrari.
   A In your dreams.
4. **A** Great shot, Charlie! Way to go!
   B Don't you wish you still played soccer?
   A Me? No. I was never any good. But *you* could have been a great player if you'd wanted.
   B Nah! I wasn't as good as Charlie. Aaah—ooh, almost! Yes!
   A Yeah, he'll go far.
5. **A** Look, I know I shouldn't have been speeding, but it was only for two minutes.
   B I've already written the ticket.
   A Come on, couldn't you look the other way? It was literally one minute.
   B One minute, two minutes. You can't break the speed limit, it's as simple as that.
   A But I just wanted to get to the drugstore before it closed. I've got to pick up a prescription for my sick grandmother. Supposing you let it go just this once.
   B I don't care what you were doing. I'm just doing my job. You've got two weeks to pay.

T 11.3

Well, Carrie and I were on vacation in Vanuatu in the South Pacific, it's really beautiful there, and uh, one day we went for a walk and saw this piece of land for sale. It was on a cliff overlooking a bay, and you can imagine—the views were absolutely fantastic. We just fell in love with it. We had to have it—and so we bought it then and there, and the next day we hired an architect to design our dream vacation home. That evening we celebrated with a lot of champagne, and in the middle of the night we were fast asleep when suddenly we were thrown from our beds. The room was shaking—it was the biggest earthquake that had ever hit the region. But the worst was still to come, because next morning when we drove out to check our newly bought land, we found that the whole cliff had fallen into the sea. It was a tragedy for us. We lost every cent we had, and our marriage never really recovered.

T 11.4

1. **A** Would it be OK if I left a little early today? I have a dental appointment.
   B No problem. Just tell Janet to cover for you.
2. **A** Win? What do you mean? If you ask me, they don't stand a chance.
   B But they've been playing much better lately, don't you think?
   A Come on. They haven't won a game in months.
3. **A** If you knew what I know, you'd never go out with him again.
   B You're just jealous.
4. **A** Could I have a word with you if you've got a minute?
   B Yeah, of course, but I'm in a bit of a rush.
   A It's about that pay raise I was promised.
5. **A** Aren't you helping Jackie plan her wedding?
   B I am. It's a nightmare. If anything went wrong, I'd never forgive myself.
6. **A** How's it going?
   B OK. If all goes well, we should be finished by Friday. We've just got to put the finishing touches on the doors and windows.
7. **A** We arrived on a Tuesday and—
   B It was a Thursday, not a Tuesday, if I remember correctly.
   A Oh Tuesday, Thursday—the day doesn't matter. I'll just never forget the blue of the water and the white of the sand.
8. **A** Well, if worst comes to worst, we can always postpone it.
   B I'd rather not. I've just got a slight headache. The sea air will do me good.
   A OK, if you're sure.
9. **A** You haven't made much progress, if any.
   B What do you mean? I've written 500 words.
   A Yeah, but you have to write 10,000.
10. **A** I don't think much of Nancy's new boyfriend. He's really cold and arrogant.
    B Actually, I don't think he's cold or arrogant. If anything, he's a little shy.
    A Shy! You wouldn't say that if you'd seen him at Ned's party!

T 11.5

1. In any relationship you have to be prepared to give and take. You can't have your own way all the time.
2. I didn't buy much at the mall. Just a few odds and ends for the kids. Socks for Ben and hairbands for Jane.
3. I'd been visiting Florida off and on for years before I finally moved there.
4. It's difficult to explain the ins and outs of the rules of baseball. It's so complicated.
5. **A** What did you get me for my birthday?
   B You'll have to wait and see.
6. **A** Oh, no! The Burtons are coming for lunch! I hate their kids!
   B I'm sorry, but you'll just have to grin and bear it. It's only for an hour or so.
7. OK, you can have it for $90. That's my final offer, take it or leave it.
8. California has lots of faults, of course, but by and large, it's a pleasant place to live.

T 11.6 See p. 110

T 11.7

Well, my story, I guess it's in the supernatural category—which is—which is strange for me because I am a very down-to-earth person. I am basically pretty skeptical when people tell weird and wonderful stories. But there is just one time when something very weird and inexplicable happened to me.
Um, it was when I was in college, a long time ago, and I had a girlfriend, and the first time I stayed at her house I had this incredibly vivid dream. You know sometimes when you wake up and you're not sure what's more real, the dream or what's around you? It was like that. Nothing very momentous happened in the dream, but in the main part of it I was walking along a street in my hometown, and I bumped into my girlfriend unexpectedly, and we stood in the street and we kissed and everyone was looking, and it was just a really strange atmosphere. Right?
And I was just lying there, in bed, and I was just thinking how incredibly vivid this dream was. I could just remember every detail of the scene. And then my girlfriend came in with a cup of tea for me. And she walked in the door and said, "Wow I had this really strange dream last night." I just knew what she was going to say, it felt like that, and she went on to describe the dream she'd had and it was *exactly* the same as the dream I'd had. And then she looked at me and she said, "What's wrong?" Because I must have looked very, very shocked. And I asked her to describe the street where we were. And she described the shop that we were standing in front of, and she said it was a stationery store. She remembered that, selling pens and paper, and stuff like that, which is exactly right. And I was feeling pretty cold and shivery by this time.
Well, the really spooky part is that I knew it was the town that I had grown up in, but at this point she'd never been there, so she didn't know the town at all, and yet she was describing it very accurately. And I was… I was kind of obsessed by this point, and I wanted to make sure that it was not just a similar street and drew this little map of the street and asked her to describe things, and she put tons of details into it—like she could say exactly where the traffic lights and the crosswalk were. So, I don't know, it must have been my dream in a way because only I knew the town, but somehow I must have transmitted it to her. It's just inexplicable. Well, I saw a TV show last year where they said that it's called "dream telepathy," and they say that it's not that unusual in dreams. Well, it's never happened to me since, and to be honest I can't say that I'd want it to, because it was actually, strangely, very disturbing.

T 11.8

1. **A** I could kick myself. As soon as I'd handed it in, I remembered what the answer was.
   B Oh, I hate it when that happens! But do you think you still passed?
2. **A** I can't believe it! I've spent all morning trying to send this, and all I get is "Oops! Your message wasn't sent. Try again later."

B What a pain! Have you tried calling the computer helpline?
3. A These instructions don't make any sense to me at all. If you can follow them, you're a genius.
   B Don't ask me! I had exactly the same trouble trying to put together a nightstand.
4. A It's not fair. I'd been looking forward to watching it all day and then the phone goes and rings!
   B Typical! And who was it? Anyone interesting?
5. A How many times do I have to tell you? Take them off *before* you come into the house!
   B Go easy on me! I was in a hurry. Anyway, they're not *that* muddy.
6. A You've got to be kidding. You promised you'd deliver it by Thursday at the latest. Now you're saying next week!
   B I'm awfully sorry, sir. I'm afraid there's nothing I can do about it. It's out of my hands.
7. A I went away to think about it, and of course, when I went back it was gone. I wish I'd just bought it then and there.
   B It's such a shame. It would have gone so well with your white jeans.
8. A What a waste of time! Ten minutes listening to music and "All our lines are busy. Thank you for waiting."
   B I know, it drives me crazy. But worse still is that you never get to speak to a real person anyway!

T 11.9 See p. 97

UNIT 12

T 12.1

My grandfather, who's a widower, used to be a judge, and when he retired the year before last, he decided to go on an ocean cruise. He enjoyed the cruise very much. He sailed all around the world and it sounded like a great experience. Anyway, the most interesting thing about this cruise was that he met an attractive widow. I think she's pretty rich, too. She's from California. Well, my grandfather invited her to have dinner with him, and they got along really well with one another. And would you believe it, my grandfather fell in love? No kidding! He says that you can find love at any age. And the next thing we knew he'd asked her to marry him. Apparently, they were married by the captain of the ship. It's so romantic. The whole family's amazed, but we're all very happy for him 'cause he's been pretty lonely since my grandmother died. I just hope I find love one day, like Grandpa.

T 12.2

1. Do any of your friends like dancing?
2. What are the people in your class like?
3. I just sent my nephew $10 for his birthday.
4. Did you know Bob's training to be a vet and he doesn't even like animals?
5. Isn't your mother Canadian?
6. What do you think the most important thing in life is?
7. I bet you've told lots of girls that you love them.
8. It's very kind of you to offer, but I can't take your car. You might have to use it this afternoon.
9. There was quite a crowd at your birthday party, wasn't there?

T 12.3

1. A Do any of your friends like dancing?
   B What do you mean, any? *All* my friends like dancing. We go every Saturday night.
2. A What are the people in your class like?
   B They're great. Every person in my class is really friendly. We all get along really well together.
3. A I just sent my nephew $10 for his birthday.
   B Well, I have five nieces. I gave $10 to each one for Christmas. And then I had nephews, cousins, in-laws, godchildren… It cost me a fortune.
   A I only have the one nephew for now. Thank goodness.
4. A Did you know Bob's training to be a vet and he doesn't even like animals?
   B That's strange. Don't you think a love of animals is vital for a vet?
   A Of course. I guess Bob wanted to be a doctor but he failed the exams.
5. A Isn't your mother Canadian?
   B Actually, *both* my parents are Canadian. My father was born in Montreal but he moved to New York when he was eighteen.
6. A What do you think the most important thing in life is?
   B I think love is everything. If you can find true love, you'll be happy forever.
7. A I bet you've told lots of girls that you love them.
   B This time it's different. The love I have for you is forever. I've never felt like this before.
8. A It's very kind of you to offer, but I can't take your car. You might have to use it this afternoon.
   B Look, I have *two* cars. Borrow either one. I don't mind. I probably won't be using either anyway.
9. A There was quite a crowd at your birthday party, wasn't there?
   B Yeah, it was great to see everyone, and I think they all had a good time.

T 12.4

1. What's that song you're singing?
2. Look at this ladybug on my hand!
3. Did you hear that storm in the middle of the night?
4. Mmm! These strawberries are delicious!
5. Take those dirty shoes off! I've just cleaned in here.
6. I can't stand this weather. It's really getting me down.
7. Who was that man you were talking to this morning?
8. Do you remember when we were young? Those were the days!
9. Children have no respect for authority these days, do they?

T 12.5

1. A What was the meal like?
   B It was disgusting, every bit as bad as you said it would be.
2. A Did you apologize to all the guests?
   B Each and every one of them. I felt like I had to.
3. A They didn't all pass, did they?
   B All but three did. Three out of 20, that's not bad.
4. A Sorry, I only have 50 cents on me.
   B Don't worry. Every little bit helps, you know.
5. A When do you think you'll get there?
   B If all goes well, we should be there about six.
6. A Want to grab a bite to eat?
   B If it's all the same to you, I'd rather not.

T 12.6

1. **Bernie**
Personally, I'm just happy to be alive. I have this enormous appetite to get everything I can out of life. I know it sounds corny, but after all that I've been through I just appreciate each day. Uh—every single day I have with my wife and kids is much more than I thought I'd have a few years ago.
It all started in my 20s—I began to feel very run-down and, being a pretty athletic person, it was clear something wasn't quite right. Anyway, I had some tests and when the results came back, the doctor walked into the room and I just knew from his face that it was something awful. Uh, I'd been diagnosed with a rare liver disease and he told me that if I didn't have a transplant I'd be dead in 18 months. I went into denial. You see, I'd recently gotten married and our baby son had just been born, and I couldn't stand the thought of him not having a father. Anyway, I had the transplant and at first everyone was very optimistic, but in fact … my body rejected the transplant and … uh … from relief I fell back into despair. I had to wait for an exact match, a matching donor to be found. It was torture not only for me but for my whole family. This time though, after the operation I knew right away it would be OK. It felt different. Eventually I started working again. These days the only thing that makes me unhappy is meeting people who don't realize what a gift life is—they just take all they have for granted. I could never do that. The birth of our daughter a year ago was just the icing on the cake for me.

2. **Hayley**
I = Interviewer   H = Hayley
I Teenagers get a bad rap, don't they?
H I know and it's so unfair—you watch TV or read the papers and it's all kids getting high on drugs and booze and stuff.
I So how do you and you friends get your kicks?
H Well, of course we like going out and having fun. We go to parties and dance and stuff…
I And drink?
H Well, actually, most of us just get off on dancing. I just love it when I'm dancing I …
I Do you have a boyfriend?
H Not right now. Life's simpler that way. I'm really happier without one. You have a boyfriend and all they ever want to do is watch football, play football, talk about football. Boring! I have really good times with my girlfriends. We do things and have real conversations.
I So what do you talk about? Boys?
H OK, yeah sometimes. But lots of things. Honestly, the best times I've had are just nights talking with my friends.
I Do any of them have boyfriends?
H Oh yeah. Some girls have to have boyfriends. You know what I mean.
I What do you mean?
H Well, you know they don't feel good about themselves unless some boy wants them. It's all they want to talk about, uh…
I And you don't like that?
H Of course not. It's pathetic. I want to do things for myself, by myself—not tie myself to one person. I had a boyfriend all last year—yeah he was cute but you can't have a relationship for life that begins when you're fifteen.
I Some people do.
H Not these days. I want to see the world, meet lots of people, get a good career before I settle down.
I Sounds exciting. Good luck with it all.

3. **Tony**
The kind of things that get me down are part political and part physical. I suppose like a lot of old, or older, people, I think the world has gone to pot. All these politicians come and go, but they don't make any difference, they all sound the same, they make promises and then break them. And then, on the physical side, I don't have the energy I used to have. I'm exhausted by lunchtime. I always seem to have aches and pains somewhere—knees, hip, shoulder, back.
The best thing I ever did was take early retirement. Honestly! It was like buying my life back. Suddenly I could do what I wanted. The first thing we did, Lizzie and me, was move to the country. We have a fantastic cottage by the sea, and we love taking our dog, Bonnie, for walks on the beach, or the cliffs, or the harbors. We have a big backyard, and there is no better feeling for me than spending the whole day outside. I like to walk around in the early morning, listening to the birds, and smelling the fresh, early-

morning air. I planted some fruit trees a year or so ago, and that's coming along well, and Lizzie and I are content just to putter in the vegetable patch, or cut the grass, or weed the flower beds. Having said that, we go out for lunch with friends pretty often, or we have friends come and stay with us for the weekend. One of my favorite things to do is to sit out on the porch in the evening and watch the sunset, with a good book.

4. **Tommy**
I = Interviewer   T = Tommy
I   So what makes you happy, Tommy?
T   Mmmm … my *best* thing is to go to Bigbury Beach.
I   Where's that?
T   It's where the sea is.
I   Nice. What do you do there?
T   I play… I play with my brother in the tide pools and we have buckets and spades and when the tide's in we go on the sea tractor and—
I   A sea tractor? What's that?
T   You know it's when the tide comes in and you can't get to the island, so you go on the sea tractor. It's got big, big wheels, hugest wheels ever.
I   Bigger than you?
T   Yeah. This big. You have to climb up the steps at the back to get on it.
I   Wow! And it goes through the water to the island?
T   Yeah. I like it. It costs 60 cents.
I   Is that right? It sounds great, Tommy, and going on the sea tractor makes you happy. So what makes you unhappy?
T   Uh … uh I think it's—it's—I think it's when birds die.
I   When *birds* die?
T   Yeah, I don't like it.
I   Have you *seen* birds die?
T   Yeah, our cat got one in the backyard and it was dead and it made me sad.
I   Ah, I see. That *is* sad when a cat catches a bird.
T   Yeah, and I saw it lying on our porch. I didn't like it.

T 12.7

1. **A** I can't believe it. I failed again.
   B Don't worry. You'll have better luck next time.
   A But that was the second time.
   B Well, maybe you'll pass next time. You know what they say—third time's the charm!
2. **A** Come on. Get up! Get a life!
   B What do you mean?
   A Well, it's high time you did something other than watch soap operas all day.
   B Like what?
   A I dunno. Travel, see the world. Live life.
   B Boring.
   A I give up. Be a couch potato if that's what you want.
3. **A** Oh no! We missed it. It must have left right on time.
   B I thought we'd just make it.
   A What do we do now? There isn't another until 1 o'clock.
   B That's nearly two hours to kill!
   A More shopping?
   B Not on your life. I'm shopped-out! Let's just get a cup of coffee. There's a cafe on platform 1.
4. **A** How's it going?
   B Well, they've finished at last but not on time—almost four weeks late.
   A And how much is it all going to cost?
   B We haven't gotten the final bill yet—
   A Well, you can bet your life it'll be more than they estimated.
   B I know. We *were* going to have the kitchen decorated too, but enough's enough for the time being.
5. **A** How come Dave has such a cushy life? He never seems to do any work.
   B Didn't you know? He won the lottery.
   A You're kidding. I had no idea. I play the lottery every week and never win a thing.
   B Me neither. But that's life.

T 12.8 That's Life

That's life, that's what people say.
You're ridin' high in April,
Shot down in May.
But I know I'm gonna change that tune,
When I'm back on top in June.
That's life, funny as it seems.
Some folks get their kicks
Steppin' on dreams;
But I don't let it get me down,
'cause this ol' world keeps spinnin' around.
I've been a puppet, a pauper, a pirate,
A poet, a pawn, and a king.
I've been up and down and over and out
And I know one thing:
Each time I find myself flat on my face,
I pick myself up and get back in the race.
That's life, I can't deny it,
I thought of quitting,
But my heart just won't buy it.
If I didn't think it was worth a try,
I'd roll myself up in a big ball and die.

T 12.9

1. **A** Did you see the game last night?
   B No, but apparently it was a good one. We won, didn't we?
   A Actually, it was a tie, but it was really exciting.
2. **A** What do you think of Claire's new boyfriend?
   B Personally, I can't stand him. I think he'll dump her like all the rest. However, that's her problem, not mine.
   A Poor old Claire! She always picks the wrong ones, doesn't she? Anyway, we'll find out soon enough.
3. **A** I don't know how you can afford to buy all those fabulous clothes!
   B Hopefully, I'm going to get a bonus this month. My boss promised. After all, I *did* earn the company over $100,000 last year. Basically, I deserve it.
4. **A** She said some terrible things to me. I hate her!
   B All the same, I think you should apologize to her. If you ask me, you lose your temper too easily. You're being very childish. It's time you both grew up!
   A What? I never thought I'd hear you speak to me like that.
   B Honestly, I'm not taking sides. I just think you should make up.
5. **A** So, Billy. You say that this is the last record you're ever going to make?
   B Definitely.
   A But surely you realize how upset your fans are going to be?
   B Obviously, I don't want to hurt anyone, but basically, I'm fed up with pop music. I'd like to do something else. Ideally, I'd like to get into movies.

This page has been left blank.

Pages 142–148 (the Grammar Reference pages for Units 1–6) appear in Student Book 4A.

Grammar Reference

UNIT 7

7.1 Introduction to modal auxiliary verbs

1 These are the modal auxiliary verbs.

can	could	may	might	should
will	would	must	ought to	

They are used with great frequency and with a wide range of meanings. They express ideas such as willingness and ability, permission and refusal, obligation and prohibition, suggestion, necessity, promise and intention. All modal auxiliary verbs can express degrees of certainty, probability, or possibility.

2 They have several characteristics.

- There is no *-s* in the third person.
  He can swim.
  She must go.

- There is no *do/does* in the question.
  May I ask a question?
  Shall we go?

- There is no *don't/doesn't* in the negative.
  You shouldn't tell lies.
  You won't believe this.

- They are followed by an infinitive without *to*. The exception is *ought to*.
  It might rain.
  Could you help?
  We ought to be on our way.

- They don't really have past forms or infinitives or *-ing* forms. Other verbs are used instead.
  I had to work hard when I was young.
  I'd love to be able to ski.
  I hate having to get up in the morning.

- They can be used with perfect infinitives to refer to the past. For more information, see Grammar Reference Unit 10 on p. 153.
  You should have told me that you can't swim.
  You might have drowned!
  She must have been crazy to marry him.

7.2 Modal auxiliary verbs of probability, present and future

The main modal auxiliary verbs that express probability are described here in order of certainty. *Will* is the most certain, and *might/could* are the least certain.

will

Will and *won't* are used to predict a future action. The truth or certainty of what is asserted is more or less taken for granted.
I'll see you later.
His latest book will be out next month.

must and can't

1 *Must* is used to assert what we infer or conclude to be the most logical or rational interpretation of a situation. We do not have all the facts, so it is less certain than *will*.
  You say he walked across the Sahara Desert! He must be crazy!
  You must be joking! I simply don't believe you.

2 The negative of this use is *can't*.
  She can't have a ten-year-old daughter! She's only twenty-one herself.
  "Whose coat is this?" "It can't be Mary's. It's too small."

should

1 *Should* expresses what may reasonably be expected to happen. Expectation means believing that things are or will be as we want them to be. This use of *should* has the idea of *if everything has gone according to plan*.
  Our guests should be here soon (if they haven't gotten lost).
  This homework shouldn't take you too long (if you've understood what you have to do).
  We should be moving into our new house soon (as long as nothing goes wrong).

2 *Should* in this use has the idea that we want the action to happen. It is not used to express negative or unpleasant ideas.
  You should pass the exam. You've worked hard.

*~~You should fail the exam~~. You haven't done any work at all.
We would say … I don't think you'll pass the exam.

may and *might*

1. *May* expresses the possibility that an event will happen or is happening.
   We **may go** to Greece this year. We haven't decided yet.
   "Where's Ann?" "She **may be taking** a bath, I don't know."
2. *Might* is more tentative and slightly less certain than *may*.
   It **might rain**. Take your umbrella.
   "Where's Peter?" "He **might be** upstairs. There's a light on."
3. Learners of English often express these concepts of future possibility with *perhaps* or *maybe* … *will* and so avoid using *may* and *might*. However, these are widely used by native speakers, and you should try to use them.

could

1. *Could* has a similar meaning to *might*.
   You **could be** right. I'm not sure.
   That movie **could be** worth seeing. It had a good review.
2. *Couldn't* is not used to express a future possibility. The negative of *could* in this use is *might not*.
   You **might not be** right.
   That movie **might not be** any good.
3. *Couldn't* has a similar meaning to *can't* above, only slightly weaker.
   She **couldn't have** a ten-year-old daughter! She's only 21 herself.

Related verbs

Here are some related verb forms that express probability.
William's so brainy. He**'s sure to pass** the exam.
We're having a picnic tomorrow, so it**'s sure to rain**.
You**'re likely to find** life very different when you live in China.
Are you **likely to come across** Judith while you're in Oxford?

7.3 Other uses of modal auxiliary verbs and related verbs

Here is some further information about modal auxiliary verbs, but it is by no means complete. See a grammar book for more details.

Ability

1. *Can* expresses ability. The past is expressed by *could*.
   I **can** speak three languages.
   I **could** swim when I was three.
2. Other forms are provided by *be able to*.
   I've never **been able to** understand her. (Present Perfect)
   I'd love **to be able to** drive. (infinitive)
   Being able to drive has transformed my life. (*-ing* form)
   You'**ll be able to** walk again soon. (future)
3. To express a fulfilled ability on one particular occasion in the past, *could* is not used. Instead, we use *was able to* or *managed to*.
   She **was able to** survive by clinging onto the wrecked boat.
   The prisoner **managed to** escape by climbing onto the roof.

Advice

1. *Should* and *ought* express mild obligation or advice. *Should* is much more common.
   You **should go** to bed. You look very tired.
   You **ought to** take things easier.
2. We use *had better* to give strong advice, or to tell people what to do. There can be an element of threat – "If you don't do this, something bad will happen."
   You'**d better** get a haircut before the interview. (If you don't, you won't get the job.)
   I'm late. I'**d better** get a move on. (If I don't, I'll be in trouble.)

Note
The form is always past (*had*), but it refers to the immediate future.
She'**d better** start revising. The exams are next week.

Obligation

1. *Must* expresses strong obligation. Other verb forms are provided by *have to*.
   You **must** try harder!
   What time **do** you **have to** start work?
   I **had to** work hard to pass my exams. (Past Simple)
   You'**ll have to** do this exercise again. (future)
   We might **have to** spend less money. (infinitive)
   She'**s never had to** do a single day's work in her life. (Present Perfect)
   I hate **having to** get up early. (*-ing* form)
2. *Must* expresses the opinion of the speaker.
   I **must** get my hair cut. (I am telling myself.)
   You **must** do this again. (Teacher to student)
   Must is associated with a more formal, written style.
   Candidates **must** answer three questions. (On an exam)
   Books **must** be returned by the end of the week. (Instructions in a library)
3. *Have to* expresses a general obligation based on a law or rule, or based on the authority of another person.
   Children **have to** go to school until they're sixteen. (It's the law.)
   Mom says you **have to** clean your room.
4. *Can't* expresses negative obligation. *Don't have to* expresses the absence of obligation.
   You **can't** steal. It's very naughty.
   You **don't have to** go to England if you want to learn English.
5. *Have got to* is more informal than *have to*.
   I'**ve got to** go now. See you!
   Don't stay out late. We'**ve got to** get up early tomorrow.
6. Here are some related verb forms that express obligation.
   Visitors **are required to** have a visa.
   When you're 18, you'**re supposed to** take responsibility for yourself.
   You **aren't supposed to** park on double yellow lines.
   You **need to** think carefully before you make a decision.
   He **doesn't need to** work. He's a millionaire.

Permission

1. *May*, *can*, and *could* are used to ask for permission.
   May I ask you a question?
   May I use your phone?
   Can/Could I go home? I don't feel well.
   Can/Could I borrow your car tonight?
2. *May* is used to give permission, but it sounds very formal. *Can* and *can't* are more common.
   You **can** use a dictionary in this exam.
   You **can't** stay up till midnight. You're only five.
   You **can't** smoke in here. It's forbidden.
3. To talk about permission generally, or permission in the past, we use *can*, *could*, or *be allowed to*.
   Children **can/are allowed to** do what they want these days.
   I **couldn't / wasn't allowed to** go out on my own until I was sixteen.
4. Here are some related verb forms that express permission.
   Passengers **are not permitted to** use cell phones.
   My parents **don't allow** me **to**
   I'm **not allowed to** stay out late.
   My parents **don't let** me
   Note that this sentence with *let* is not possible in the passive.
   *~~I'm not let~~ …

Willingness and refusal

1 *Will* expresses willingness. *Won't* expresses a refusal by either people or things. *Shall* is used in questions.
I'll help you.
She says she **won't** get up until she's had breakfast in bed.
The car **won't** start.
Shall I give you a hand?

2 The past is expressed by *wouldn't*.
My mum said she **wouldn't** give me any more money. Isn't she mean?

Requests

Several modal verbs express a request.
Can/could/will/would *you do me a favor?*
Can/could *I open the window?*
Modal verbs are also dealt with in Units 9, 10, and 11.

UNIT 8

8.1 Introduction to relative clauses

It is important to understand the difference between two kinds of relative clauses.

1 Defining relative (DR) clauses qualify a noun, and tell us exactly which person or thing is being referred to.
*She likes people **who are fun to be with**.*
*Politicians **who tell lies** are odious.*
*A corkscrew is a thing **you use to open a bottle of wine**.*
She likes people on its own doesn't mean very much; we need to know which people she likes.
who tell lies tells us exactly which politicians are odious. Without it, the speaker is saying that all politicians are odious.
A corkscrew is a thing doesn't make sense on its own.

2 Non-defining relative (NDR) clauses add secondary information to a sentence, almost as an afterthought.
*My friend Andrew, **who is Scottish**, plays the bagpipes.*
*Politicians, **who tell lies**, are odious.*
*My favorite building is Durham Cathedral, **which took over 200 years to build**.*
My friend Andrew is clearly defined. We don't need to know which Andrew is being discussed. The clause *who is Scottish* gives us extra information about him.
The clause *who tell lies* suggests that all politicians tell lies. It isn't necessary to identify only those that deceive – they all do!
My favorite building is clearly defined. The following clause simply tells us something extra.

3 DR clauses are much more common in the spoken language, and NDR clauses are more common in the written language. In the spoken language, we can avoid a NDR clause.
My friend Andrew plays the bagpipes. He's Scottish, by the way.

4 When we speak, there is no pause before or after a DR clause, and no commas when we write. With NDR clauses, there are commas before and after, and pauses when we speak.
I like the things you say to me. (No commas, no pauses)
My aunt (pause)*, who has been a widow for twenty years* (pause)*, loves traveling.*

Defining relative clauses

1 Notice how we can leave out the relative pronoun if it is the object of the relative clause. This is very common.
Pronoun left out
Did you like the present ( ) I gave you?
Who was that man ( ) you were talking to?
The thing ( ) I like about Dave is his sense of humor.

2 We cannot leave out the pronoun if it is the subject of the clause.
Pronoun not left out
*I met a man **who** works in advertising.*
*I'll lend you the book **that** changed my life.*
*The thing **that** helped me most was knowing I wasn't alone.*

3 Here are the possible pronouns. The words in brackets are possible, but not as common. ____ means "nothing."

	Person	Thing
Subject	who (that)	that (which)
Object	____ (that)	____ (that)

Notes

- *That* is preferred to *which* after superlatives, and words such as *all*, *every(thing)*, *some(thing)*, *any(thing)*, and *only*.
  *That's the **funniest** movie **that** was ever made.*
  All that's left is a few slices of ham.
  *Give me **something that**'ll take away the pain.*
  *He's good at **any** sport **that** is played with a ball.*
  *The **only** thing **that**'ll help you is rest.*

- *That* is also preferred after *it is ...*
  *It is a movie **that** will be very popular.*

- Prepositions usually come at the end of the relative clause.
  *Come and meet the people I work **with**.*
  *This is the book I was telling you **about**.*
  *She's a friend I can always rely **on**.*

Non-defining relative clauses

1 Relative pronouns *cannot* be left out of NDR clauses.
Relative pronoun as subject
*Paul Jennings, **who** has written several books, addressed the meeting.*
*His last book, **which** received a lot of praise, has been a great success.*
Relative pronoun as object
*Paul Jennings, **who** I knew in college, addressed the meeting.*
*His last book, **which** I couldn't understand at all, has been a great success.*

2 Look at the possible pronouns. *Whom* is possible, but not as common.

	Person	Thing
Subject	... , who ... ,	... , which ... ,
Object	... , who (whom) ... ,	... , which ... ,

Note
Prepositions can come at the end of the clause.
*He talked about theories of market forces, which I'd never even heard **of**.*
In a more formal written style, prepositions come before the pronoun.
*The privatization of railways, **to which** the present government is committed, is not universally popular.*

which

Which can be used in NDR clauses to refer to the whole of the sentence before.
*She arrived on time, **which** amazed everybody.*
*He gambled away all his money, **which** I thought was ridiculous.*
*The coffee machine isn't working, **which** means we can't have any coffee.*

whose

Whose can be used in both DR clauses and NDR clauses.
*That's the woman **whose** son was killed recently.*
*My parents, **whose** only interest is gardening, never go away on vacation.*

what

What is used in DR clauses to mean *the thing that*.
*Has she told you **what**'s worrying her?*
What *I need to know is where we're meeting.*

why, when, where

1. *Why* can be used in DR clauses to mean *the reason why*.
   *I don't know **why** we're arguing.*
2. *When* and *where* can be used in DR clauses and NDR clauses.
   *Tell me **when** you expect to arrive.*
   *The hotel **where** we stayed was excellent.*
   *We go walking on Mondays, **when** the rest of the world is working.*
   *He works in Baltimore, **where** my sister lives.*

8.2 Participles

1. When present participles (*-ing*) are used like adjectives or adverbs, they are active in meaning.
   *Modern art is **interesting**.*
   *Pour **boiling** water onto the pasta.*
   *She sat in the corner **crying**.*
2. When past participles (*-ed*) are used like adjectives or adverbs, they are passive in meaning.
   *I'm **interested** in modern art.*
   *Look at that **broken** doll.*
   *He sat in his chair, **filled** with horror at what he had just seen.*
3. Participles after a noun define and identify in the same way as relative clauses.
   *I met a woman **riding** a donkey.* (= who was riding …)
   *The car **stolen** in the night was later found abandoned.* (= that was stolen …)
4. Participles can be used as adverbs. They can describe:
   - two actions happening at the same time.
     *She sat by the fire **reading** a book.*
   - two actions that happen one after another.
     ***Opening** his case, he took out a gun.*
     If it is important to show that the first action is completed before the second action begins, we use the perfect participle.
     ***Having finished** lunch, we set off on our journey.*
     ***Having had** a shower, she got dressed.*
   - two actions that happen one because of another.
     ***Being** stingy, he never bought anyone a Christmas present.*
     ***Not knowing** what to do, I waited patiently.*
5. Many verbs are followed by -*ing* forms.
   *I **spent** the vacation **reading**.*
   *Don't **waste** time **thinking** about the past.*
   *Let's **go swimming**.*
   *He **keeps on asking** me to go out with him.*

UNIT 9

9.1 Expressing habit

Present Simple

1. Adverbs of frequency come before the main verb, but after the verb *to be*.
   *We **hardly ever** go out.*
   *She **frequently** forgets what she's doing.*
   *We don't **usually** eat fish.*
   *I **rarely** see Peter these days.*
   *We are **seldom** at home in the evening.*
   *Is he **normally** so bad-tempered?*
2. *Sometimes*, *usually*, and *occasionally* can come at the beginning or the end of a sentence.
   ***Sometimes** we play cards.*
   *We go to the movies **occasionally**.*
   The other adverbs of frequency don't usually move in this way.
   **Always I have* tea in the morning.*

Present Continuous

1. The Present Continuous can be used to express a habit which happens often and perhaps unexpectedly. It happens more than is usual.
   *I like Peter. He's always **smiling**.*
   *She's always **giving** people presents.*
2. However, there is often an element of criticism with this structure. Compare these sentences said by a teacher.
   *Pedro always **asks** questions in class.* (This is a fact.)
   *Pedro **is always asking** questions in class.* (This annoys the teacher.)
3. There is usually an adverb of frequency with this use.
   *I'm always **losing** my keys.*
   *She's forever **leaving** the water running.*

will and *would*

1. *Will* and *would* express typical behavior. They describe both pleasant and unpleasant habits.
   *He'**ll** sit in his chair for hours on end.*
   *She'**d** spend all day long gossiping with the neighbors.*
   Would cannot be used to express a state.
   **He'd live in a large house.*
2. *Will* and *would*, when decontracted and stressed, express an annoying habit.
   *He **WILL** come into the house with his muddy boots on.*
   *She **WOULD** make us wash in ice-cold water.*

used to + infinitive

1. This structure expresses a past action and/or a state. It has no present equivalent.
   *When I was a child, we **used to go** on vacation to Florida.* (action)
   *He **used to live** in a large house.* (state)
2. Notice the negative and the question.
   *Where **did** you **use to** go?*
   *We **didn't use to** do anything interesting.*
3. We cannot use *used to* with a time reference + a number.
   **We used to have a holiday there for 10 years/three times.*
   But …
   *We **used to** go there every year.*

be/get used to + noun + *-ing* form

1. This is totally different from *used to* + infinitive. It expresses an action that was difficult, strange, or unusual before, but is no longer so. Here, *used* is an adjective, and it means *familiar with*.
   *I found it difficult to get around New York when I first came, but I'**m used to it** now.*
   *I'**m used to getting** around New York by subway.*
2. Notice the use of *get* to express the process of change.
   *I'**m getting used to** the climate.*
   *Don't worry. You'**ll get used to** eating with chopsticks.*

UNIT 10

10.1 Modal auxiliary verbs 2

Modal auxiliary verbs of probability in the past

1. All modal auxiliary verbs can be used with the perfect infinitive. They express the same varying degrees of certainty as explained on p. 149. Again, *must have* is the most certain, and *might/may/could have* is the least certain.
   *It **must have been** a good party. Everyone stayed till dawn.*
   *The music **can't have been** any good. Nobody danced.*
   *Where's Pete? He **should have been** here ages ago!*
   *He **may have gotten** lost.*
   *He **might have decided** not to come.*

152 Grammar Reference

*He **could have been** in an accident.*

2 ***Would have thought*** is common to express an assumption or supposition.
***I'd have thought** they'd be here by now. Where are they?*
*You**'d have thought** she'd remember my birthday, wouldn't you?*
***Wouldn't** you **have thought** they'd call if there was a problem?*

Other uses of modal verbs in the past

should have

1 *Should have* can express advice or criticism about a past event. The sentence expresses what is contrary to the facts.
*You **should have listened** to my advice.* (You didn't listen.)
*I **shouldn't have lied** to you. I'm sorry.* (I did lie.)
*You **shouldn't have told** her you hated her.* (You did tell her.)

2 Look at these sentences.
*You **should have been** here yesterday!*
*You **should have seen** his face!*
Should have is used here for comic effect. The suggestion is *because it was so funny!*

3 *Shouldn't have* also expresses an action that was done, but it wasn't necessary. It was a waste of time.
*I **shouldn't have gotten up** so early. The train was delayed.*
"I've bought you a new pen, because I lost yours." "You **shouldn't have bothered**. I've got hundreds."

could have

1 *Could have* is used to express an unrealized past ability. Someone was able to do something in the past, but didn't do it.
*I **could have gone** to college, but I didn't want to.*
*We **could have won** the match. We didn't try hard enough.*
*I **could have told** you that Chris wouldn't come. He hates parties.*
*I was so angry with her, I **could have killed** her!*

2 It is used to express a past possibility that didn't happen.
*You fool! You **could have killed** yourself!*
*We were lucky. We **could have been caught** in that traffic jam.*
*When I took the burned meal out of the oven, I **could have cried**!*

3 It is used to criticize people for not doing things.
*You **could have told** me that Sue and Jim had split up!*
*I've been cleaning the house for hours. You **could** at least **have cleaned** your bedroom!*

might have

1 The above use of *should have* can also be expressed with *might have*.
*You **might have helped** instead of just sitting on your backside!*

2 *I might have known/guessed that ...* is used to introduce a typical action of someone or something.
*I **might have known** that Peter would be late. He's always late.*
*The car won't start. I **might have guessed** that would happen.*

UNIT 11

11.1 Hypothesizing

First and second conditionals

1 First conditional sentences are based on fact in real time. They express a possible condition and its probable result in the present or future.
*If you **pass** your exams, I**'ll buy** you a car.*

2 Second conditional sentences are not based on fact. They express a situation which is contrary to reality in the present and future. This unreality is shown by a tense shift from present to past. They express a hypothetical condition and its probable result.
*If I **were** taller, I**'d join** the police force.*
*What **would** you **do** if you **won** the lottery?*

Notes

- The difference between first and second conditional sentences is not about time. Both can refer to the present and future. By using past tense forms in the second conditional, the speaker suggests the situation is less probable, or impossible, or imaginary. Compare the pairs of sentences.
*If it **rains** this weekend, we**'ll** ...* (said in England where it often rains)
*If it **rained** in the Sahara, it **would** ...* (this would be most unusual)
*If global warming **continues**, we**'ll** ...* (I'm a pessimist.)
*If global warming **continued**, we**'d** ...* (I'm an optimist.)
*If you **come** to my country, you**'ll have** a good time.* (possible)
*If you **came** from my country, you**'d understand** us better.* (impossible)
*If I **am elected** as a member of Parliament, I**'ll** ...* (said by a candidate)
*If I **ruled** the world, I**'d** ...* (imaginary)

- We can use *were* instead of *was*, especially in a formal style.
*If the situation **were** the opposite, would you feel obliged to help?*
*I'd willingly help if it **were** possible.*

Third conditional

1 Third conditional sentences are not based on fact. They express a situation which is contrary to reality in the past. This unreality is shown by a tense shift from past to Past Perfect.
*If you**'d come** to the party, you**'d have had** a great time.*
*I **wouldn't have met** my wife if I **hadn't gone** to France.*

2 It is possible for each of the clauses in a conditional sentence to have a different time reference, and the result is a mixed conditional.
*If we **had brought** a map (we didn't), we **would know** where we are (we don't).*
*I **wouldn't have married** her (I did) if I **didn't love** her (I do).*

Other structures that express hypothesis

1 The tense usage with *wish*, *if only*, and *I'd rather* is similar to the second and third conditionals. Unreality is expressed by a tense shift.
*I wish I **were** taller.* (But I'm not.)
*If only you **hadn't said** that!* (But you did.)
*I'd rather you **didn't wear** lots of make-up.* (But you do.)
I'd rather you ... is often used as a polite way to tell someone to do something differently. The negative form *I'd rather you didn't ...* is especially useful as a polite way to say "no."
"I'll come in with you." "*I'd rather you **waited** outside.*"
"Can I smoke in here?" "*I'd rather you **didn't**.*"

Notes

- *wish ... would* can express regret, dissatisfaction, impatience, or irritation because someone WILL keep doing something.
*I wish you**'d stop** smoking.*
*I wish you**'d do** more to help in the house.*
*I wish it **would stop** raining.*

- If we are not talking about willingness, *wish ... would* is not used.
*I wish my birthday **wasn't** in December.* (*I wish it would be ...*)
*I wish I **could** stop smoking.* (*I wish I would* is strange because you should have control over what you are willing to do.)
*I wish **he** would stop smoking.*
This is correct because it means *I wish he were willing to ...*

UNIT 12

12.1 Determiners

There are two kinds of determiners.
1 The first kind identifies things.
   articles – *a/an, the*
   possessives – *my, your, our* …
   demonstratives – *this, that, these, those*
2 The second kind are quantifiers, expressing *how much* or *how many*.
   some, any, no
   each, every, either, neither
   much, many, more, most
   (a) little, less, least
   (a) few, fewer, fewest
   enough, several
   all, both, half
   another, other
   Determiners that express quantity are dealt with in Unit 6.

each and every

1 *Each* and *every* are used with singular nouns. *Each* can be used to talk about two or more people or things. *Every* is used to talk about three or more.
   Every/each *time I come to your house it looks different.*
   Each/every *bedroom in our hotel is decorated differently.*
2 In many cases, *each* and *every* can both be used with little difference in meaning.
   We prefer *each* if we are thinking of people or things separately, one at a time. We use *every* if we are thinking of the things or people all together as a group.
   Each *student gave the teacher a present.*
   Every *policeman in the country is looking for the killer.*

enough

1 When *enough* is used as a determiner, it comes before the noun.
   We haven't got **enough food**.
2 When it is used as an adverb, it comes after the adjective, adverb, or verb.
   Your homework isn't **good enough**.
   I couldn't run **fast enough**.
   You don't **exercise enough**.

Articles

The use of articles is complex as there are a lot of "small" rules and exceptions. Here are the basic rules.

a/an

1 We use *a/an* to refer to a singular countable noun which is indefinite. Either we don't know which one, or it doesn't matter which one.
   They live in **a** *lovely house.*
   I'm reading **a** *good book.*
   She's expecting **a** *baby.*
2 We use *a/an* with professions.
   She's **a** *lawyer.*

the

1 We use *the* before a singular or plural noun, when both the speaker and the listener know which noun is being referred to.
   They live in **the** *green house opposite* **the** *library.*
   The *book was recommended by a friend.*
   Watch **the** *baby! She's near* **the** *fire.*
   I'm going to **the** *mall. Do you want anything?*
   I'll see you in **the** *bar later.*
   "Where's Dad?" "In **the** *garden."*

2 We use *the* when there is only one.
   the *world*   **the** *River Thames*   **the** *Atlantic*
3 We use *the* for certain places which are institutions. Which particular place isn't important.
   We went to **the movies/theater** *last night.*
   We're going to **the seaside**.

a followed by the

We use *a* to introduce something for the first time. When we refer to it again, we use *the*.
I saw **a** *man walking* **a** *dog in the park today.* **The** *man was tiny and* **the** *dog was huge!*

Zero article

1 We use no article with plural and uncountable nouns when talking about things in general.
   Computers *have changed our lives.*
   Love *is eternal.*
   Dogs *need a lot of exercise.*
   I hate **hamburgers**.
2 We use no article with meals.
   Have you had **lunch** *yet?*
   Come around for **dinner** *tonight.*
   But … We had **a lovely lunch** *in an Italian restaurant.*

Appendix 1

IRREGULAR VERBS

Base form	Past Simple	Past Participle	Base form	Past Simple	Past Participle
be	was/were	been	lend	lent	lent
beat	beat	beaten	let	let	let
become	became	become	lie	lay	lain
begin	began	begun	light	lighted/lit	lighted/lit
bend	bent	bent	lose	lost	lost
bite	bit	bitten	make	made	made
blow	blew	blown	mean	meant	meant
break	broke	broken	meet	met	met
bring	brought	brought	must	had to	had to
build	built	built	pay	paid	paid
burst	burst	burst	put	put	put
buy	bought	bought	quit	quit	quit
can	could	been able	read /rid/	read /rɛd/	read /rɛd/
catch	caught	caught	ride	rode	ridden
choose	chose	chosen	ring	rang	rung
come	came	come	rise	rose	risen
cost	cost	cost	run	ran	run
cut	cut	cut	say	said	said
dig	dug	dug	see	saw	seen
do	did	done	sell	sold	sold
draw	drew	drawn	send	sent	sent
drink	drank	drunk	set	set	set
drive	drove	driven	shake	shook	shaken
eat	ate	eaten	shine	shone	shone
fall	fell	fallen	shoot	shot	shot
feed	fed	fed	show	showed	shown
feel	felt	felt	shut	shut	shut
fight	fought	fought	sing	sang	sung
find	found	found	sink	sank	sunk
fit	fit	fit	sit	sat	sat
fly	flew	flown	sleep	slept	slept
forget	forgot	forgotten	slide	slid	slid
forgive	forgave	forgiven	speak	spoke	spoken
freeze	froze	frozen	spend	spent	spent
get	got	gotten	spread	spread	spread
give	gave	given	stand	stood	stood
go	went	gone	steal	stole	stolen
grow	grew	grown	stick	stuck	stuck
hang	hung	hung	sweep	swept	swept
have	had	had	swim	swam	swum
hear	heard	heard	take	took	taken
hide	hid	hidden	teach	taught	taught
hit	hit	hit	tear	tore	torn
hold	held	held	tell	told	told
hurt	hurt	hurt	think	thought	thought
keep	kept	kept	throw	threw	thrown
kneel	knelt	knelt	understand	understood	understood
know	knew	known	wake	woke	woken
lay	laid	laid	wear	wore	worn
lead	led	led	win	won	won
leave	left	left	write	wrote	written

Appendix 2

VERB PATTERNS

Verbs + *to* + infinitive only	
agree choose dare decide expect forget help hope learn manage need offer promise refuse seem want would like would love would prefer would hate	to do to come to cook

Notes
1. *Help* and *dare* can be used without *to*.
    We **helped clean up** the kitchen.
    They didn't **dare disagree** with him.
2. *Have to* for obligation.
    I **have to wear** a uniform.
3. *Used to* for past habits.
    I **used to smoke**, but I quit last year.

Verbs + *-ing* only	
adore enjoy adore hate don't mind finish look forward to	doing swimming cooking

Note
We often use the verb *go* + *-ing* for sports and activities.
   I **go swimming** every day.
   I **go shopping** on weekends.

Verbs + *-ing* or *to* + infinitive	
(with little or no change in meaning)	
like love prefer hate can't stand begin start continue	doing to do

Verbs + *-ing* or *to* + infinitive	
(with a change in meaning)	
remember stop try	doing to do

Notes
1. I **remember mailing** the letter.
      (= I have a memory now of a past action: mailing the letter.)
   I **remembered to mail** the letter.
      (= I reminded myself to mail the letter. I didn't forget.)
2. I **stopped drinking** coffee.
      (= I gave up the habit.)
   I **stopped to drink** a coffee.
      (= I stopped doing something else in order to have a cup of coffee.)
3. I **tried to** sleep.
      (= I wanted to sleep, but it was difficult.)
   I **tried counting** sheep and **drinking** a glass of warm milk.
      (= These were possible ways of getting to sleep.)

Verbs + somebody + *to* + infinitive		
advise allow ask beg encourage expect help need invite order remind tell want warn (+ *not*) would like	me him them someone	to do to go to come

Note
Help can be used without *to*.
   I **helped** him **do** the dishes.

Verbs + somebody + infinitive (without *to*)		
let make help	her us	do

Notes
1. *To* is used with *make* in the passive.
    We were **made to work** hard.
2. *Let* cannot be used in the passive. *Allowed to* is used instead.
    She was **allowed to leave**.

Phonetic Symbols

Consonants

1	/p/	as in	**pen** /pɛn/
2	/b/	as in	**big** /bɪg/
3	/t/	as in	**tea** /ti/
4	/d/	as in	**do** /du/
5	/k/	as in	**cat** /kæt/
6	/g/	as in	**go** /goʊ/
7	/f/	as in	**five** /faɪv/
8	/v/	as in	**very** /ˈvɛri/
9	/s/	as in	**son** /sʌn/
10	/z/	as in	**zoo** /zu/
11	/l/	as in	**live** /lɪv/
12	/m/	as in	**my** /maɪ/
13	/n/	as in	**nine** /naɪn/
14	/h/	as in	**happy** /hæpi/
15	/r/	as in	**red** /rɛd/
16	/y/	as in	**yes** /yɛs/
17	/w/	as in	**want** /wɑnt/
18	/θ/	as in	**thanks** /θæŋks/
19	/ð/	as in	**the** /ðə/
20	/ʃ/	as in	**she** /ʃi/
21	/ʒ/	as in	**television** /ˈtɛlɪvɪʒn/
22	/tʃ/	as in	**child** /tʃaɪld/
23	/dʒ/	as in	**Japan** /dʒəˈpæn/
24	/ŋ/	as in	**English** /ˈɪŋglɪʃ/

Vowels

25	/i/	as in	**see** /si/
26	/ɪ/	as in	**his** /hɪz/
27	/ɛ/	as in	**ten** /tɛn/
28	/æ/	as in	**stamp** /stæmp/
29	/ɑ/	as in	**father** /ˈfɑðər/
30	/ɔ/	as in	**saw** /sɔ/
31	/ʊ/	as in	**book** /bʊk/
32	/u/	as in	**you** /yu/
33	/ʌ/	as in	**sun** /sʌn/
34	/ə/	as in	**about** /əˈbaʊt/
35	/eɪ/	as in	**name** /neɪm/
36	/aɪ/	as in	**my** /maɪ/
37	/ɔɪ/	as in	**boy** /bɔɪ/
38	/aʊ/	as in	**how** /haʊ/
39	/oʊ/	as in	**go** /goʊ/
40	/ər/	as in	**bird** /bərd/
41	/ɪr/	as in	**near** /nɪr/
42	/ɛr/	as in	**hair** /hɛr/
43	/ɑr/	as in	**car** /kɑr/
44	/ɔr/	as in	**more** /mɔr/
45	/ʊr/	as in	**tour** /tʊr/